No More Than I Can Bear

by

Natalie Thomas
with Gaylynne Sword

I dedicate this book to the most precious kids ever. Krystal, Loren, Erika, Vic and Kelli, my heart bursts with love for you guys. You make me laugh, cry, wish, and wonder all at the same time. You all are the greatest blessings that God has granted to me. When He gave you all to me, He gave me His absolute best. You have inspired me to live, love, fight, and persevere.

As I watch you all grow, I see that you have an uncanny sense of what is true, and good. Your hearts are so right and you all have such a spiritual sense of who God is.

Never doubt your wonderful God-given abilities. You have been given so much. God doesn't doubt you and neither do I. Be the doctors, teachers and personal chefs that you want to be. Do it all in His name.

Don't allow challenges and difficulties to diminish your potential. Rise up from the trials in your life and be wiser, stronger and more determined than ever. God has made each of you great, because He expects great things. You are the only ones who can limit your own potential. I believe in each of you because I know who you are and what you can be. You are wonderful children who will be great adults and have so much to contribute to the world.

Never forget to love and encourage each other. Always be there for each other. Be constant prayer warriors for the welfare of your siblings, and best friends forever to each other. Together, you have unlimited strength. Appreciate the strengths in each other and help each other through the weaknesses. Treasure your siblings — God has given you an awesome gift - each other.

You are the best and you deserve the best.

Thanks for loving me unconditionally and for allowing me the honor to be a mother to the five brightest jewels ever. I adore you all. I love you with all my heart. May my love wrap around you forever.

No matter what, I am only a prayer away.

Acknowledgments

I appreciate the following family, friends, and organizations for their encouragement, support, understanding and love during the events that have led to the writing of this book:

John and Alfreda Cunningham - my parents, thank you for everything, for so many years. I love you.

The Baxter Family - I'll never forget any of you.

The First Academy - an abundance of thanks to the faculty, staff and parents for all that you do.

First Baptist of Orlando, First Baptist of Windermere, and Fellowship Orlando - you are awesome examples for the Christian community.

Gaylynne Sword - thanks for a job well done.

The Bristol Connection and Uncle Ras - thanks for the love of family.

Ned McLeod and Nik Nikic- thanks for your professional advice and belief in this project.

The Athletic Staff at TFA - thanks for nurturing my "Future Royals."

Contributors to the trust fund - where would we be without you? You made such a difference in our lives, thank-you for caring. How do we thank you?

Julie Jancek - thanks for your time and energy

Brenda, Cody, Don and Sharen, Don and Sheri, Donna, Ed, Gina, Glenn and Cheryl, Gloria, Kathy, Renee, Shaun, and Tanya - I don't know what I did to deserve friends like you, but I'm sure glad God put you in my life. You were a safe harbor when I felt I had no other.

My girlfriends who allowed me to bend their ear over and over - XXOO

To the readers - you are so gracious to allow my journey to temporarily become a part of yours.

Table of Contents

Prologue

"Come straight home," she said.

It was around 3:30 pm on a cool early spring afternoon. The date was March 2, the day after my middle daughter's birthday. I was driving along with my kids after picking them up from school when the cell phone rang. My mother had been visiting for a few days and was supposed to have gone home the day before, but had a premonition that she needed to stay. I answered the phone to hear my mother's voice asking if I was coming straight home. I replied that I was. She ended the brief conversation, repeating again, "Come straight home."

I was a little puzzled at her tone, but said, "Okay, I'll be there after I run over to a friend's to get Krystal. She is excited about going to a party tonight and we need to get right home." My mother didn't seem interested in all the particulars, which surprised me. Again, her firm request was, "Just be sure you get here as soon as you can, and don't stop anywhere."

"Is everything okay?" I inquired.

"When will you get here?" she asked.

I assured her that I would get there in the next 15 minutes.

In the meantime, I had been listening to the radio and heard of a bad accident on John Young Parkway. " Oh no," I thought. That was the direction that Victor was headed on the way to his mandatory captain's meeting. I knew what was going on, no one wanted to tell me that he'd been killed. I just knew he was in that accident. This was the type of call that wives of law enforcement officers completely dread and halfway expect. It had a menacing aura and provoked a feeling of impending doom. In the back of our minds at all times were the nagging "what-ifs" inherent to living with a man whose profession demanded he spend the day looking over his shoulder and touting firearms, trying to uphold peace and justice.

When I hung up the phone, I knew that Capt. Victor Thomas, my husband, was dead and no one wanted to break the news to me while I was driving. Had my fear become a reality? I had practiced the thought for years, especially since he had spent so many years in the undercover drug unit. So, when my mother called back about fifteen minutes later, I held my breath and asked again, "Mama, please just tell me . . . is Victor dead?"

My life as I knew it was about to die. We all were about to be cast in our own tragic melodrama, having no knowledge of how it would end. As I drove the last few miles to our home, I couldn't imagine that the mirror which reflected my vision of life would be shattered into many painful, piercing shards. I would have to tread carefully as I walked and learned to move on. And little did I know, but I was in for the fight of my life.

CHAPTER 1

The World at Our Feet

"The man who finds a wife finds a treasure and receives
favor from the Lord."

Proverbs 18:22

It was a Wednesday morning, one of those sunny, winter
days that makes you love living in Florida. The weather
was just perfect. Even though I had completed a bachelor's
degree at another college, it was my first day of the 1980
winter semester at the University of Central Florida. He
came strolling out of the engineering building, all six-foot-
five-inch, fit, trim, and slightly handsome of him. Our eyes
met. "Hmm, a little thin, I thought to myself, but nice legs."
Definitely, attraction at first sight, you might say, Victor
Thomas. A little inner voice told me that this man was going
to be significant in my life.

We didn't talk then.

On Friday, the same thing happened, but this time he
was passing out flyers advertising his fraternity's party. He

shyly came over and handed me one. Then we briefly talked about the plans for the party and the directions to the location. Well, I knew better than to go to any fraternity party on the first invitation and especially with people I didn't know.

Nevertheless, I gave him the impression that I was going to come, which seemed to please him. But I knew my real plan was to go home to visit my parents that weekend.

My parents lived in our hometown of Winter Haven — a moderate sized city about an hour away from Orlando. They still lived in the same house where I grew up and I enjoyed going home. My parents weren't by any means wealthy, but had managed their few resources well enough to provide a comfortable living for themselves and me. They seemed to have had a fulfilling and supportive marriage for almost 50 years.

My family had taken a firm stand on social concerns throughout my formative years. They sent a strong message about loyalty and fidelity in marriages and set an example for me that, even though it might not be easy, your first responsibility is to work it out. I had an uncle who had married the same woman twice, and another uncle who fought through a tough time in his marriage. When my cousin got pregnant, she got married. I had witnessed my own mother and father go through tension filled times, and they were able to work things out to keep stability in our home. Marriage, kids, and trust were no trivial matter to my family, and I grew up with a strong sense of what I envisioned a marriage to be. My mother had always shown undying loyalty to my father. In retrospect, I think Victor was attracted to these values.

My parents were involved in my life, but my relationship with my father was always special. My mother told stories of me riding in the car, back in the days when seatbelts weren't required, and I would stand beside my father in the front seat with my arm around his neck as we rode. I went everywhere with him. As I got older, our father daughter talks often focused on independence. He placed a great deal of importance on that. He would say that because I was an only child, it was important for me to be able to provide a good life for myself.

I'm sure that I developed a trust of men because I could always trust my father. There was never any doubt that my father was there for me, as was my mother. Above all, my father and I were more kindred spirits.

* * *

"How was the party?" I asked when he came out of the engineering auditorium on Monday morning. "Good," he said, "Why didn't you come?" I told him I had gone home for the weekend. We continued to talk for a short time before my class started. These meetings became a habit until we finally exchanged phone numbers and addresses. Could we ever have guessed that this bit of flirting was forging a seven-year courtship?

Things couldn't have been more perfect. This prince seemed to be searching for a princess and he had chosen me. He was even willing to wait for me while I ended another long-term relationship. He would sit in my apartment as my current boyfriend and I would talk on the phone and even saw flowers in the apartment from him. I'd ask him why he was willing to sit around and watch all this and he would confidently reply, "I know if I wait long enough, I'll win." At the time I really didn't understand him, and I thought this was a little odd, but I was certainly flattered by his persistence. Eventually the other relationship did end. Victor won. We immediately became inseparable, even scheduling classes together whenever possible.

He had a special whistle I'd often hear while walking across campus. Sometimes I couldn't even see where he was, but when I heard that high-pitched shrill, I'd strain my eyes to see **where** it was coming from. I instinctively knew **who** it was coming from. Soon, I'd see this tall, lean figure waving his arms and smiling. It was comforting to know that he was thinking about me, and I knew beyond a shadow of a doubt that whatever else was going on in his life, it was getting second best, because I was getting first.

He was quite chivalrous and protective. If a guy used profanity around me, he'd make him apologize. If there were doors to be opened, he'd open them for me. He knew how to take care of me. Many times he anticipated my needs before I ever thought of them. I also took my turns at taking care of him. Once, early in our relationship, he had eleven teeth extracted, and I played nurse, changing the saliva soaked, bloody gauzes that plugged the holes in his gums. He, like most men, was not a good patient, but caring for him gave me a great sense of satisfaction.

Our favorite date was a movie and pizza from the nearby Pizza Hut. Occasionally, we'd go out to area nightclubs for a few dances and drinks. I loved to dance with him. I could feel the strength in his arms even then. We weren't big into partying, we just liked to be social. He was very active in the campus Black Student Union (B.S.U.), and they often had parties to raise money. When we went to fraternity and B.S.U. parties, Victor usually worked the door. He would stand there to collect money and maintain order, which didn't take much with this big impressive man standing there.

He liked the position of trust and responsibility. Victor also made me feel safe when I was around him.

After graduation, we had the world at our feet. I began working as a medical technologist in the laboratory at the local hospital. Victor entered the police academy and embarked on his 18-year career with the Orange County Sheriff's department, seven of which were spent in the undercover drug unit.

In the early years of his job, he got permission for me to ride with him. After two nights of riding, I thought, "This has to be the most boring job ever created." The thing we did the most on these nights — drive, drive, drive. While driving, Victor would tell me which cops slept on the job, which cops visited their girlfriends while on duty and which cops diverted calls to fellow officers. He also made a point to show me which officers had given him a hard time when he was a Field Training Officer (F.T.O.), believing he wouldn't make a good cop. I knew he was determined to prove them wrong.

My parents had come to love Victor like a son. He became our family. When we went to Tennessee for Christmas with our family, Victor went too. When my father went to homecoming at his alma mater of Hampton University, Victor went along. My parents and extended family accepted him as if they had known him all our lives. It didn't take long for them to grow to love him and he seemed to welcome that. He wanted that. It was an easy fit, a comfortable fit. He especially loved helping my parents, and they loved helping him. They trusted him.

In those days, we were ambitious and free to do pretty much whatever we wanted. With two full-time salaries, and practically no debts, we had money to travel, have elegant dinners, shop, and invest. It was a very giving relationship, both giving of ourselves and our resources to please the other. Although Victor was never one to spend money frivolously, he was generous and thoughtful. Downright romantic . . .

In fact, he often brought me flowers, just because, or took me to dinner when we were in the mood for something different. We took delight in planning fancy vacations together. I got the feeling that this was his first experience planning multifaceted trips across the country and even out of the country. We traveled to the Bahamas, the Virgin Islands and Hawaii to enjoy the sun and surf. We went to San Francisco, the Grand Canyon and Las Vegas, where we saw the sights, tasted fine wines, and strolled around at the spectacular hotels. Our favorite vacation spot was Lake Tahoe, California or Nevada, depending on which side of the state line we vacationed on. Our days were spent skiing the slopes of the Sierra mountains and our evenings were spent trying our luck in the casinos, before retiring to our lodge. We always made sure we had a fireplace in the cabin. We loved to sit in front of the fire with a glass of wine, listening to the crackle of the fire while watching the snow fall. The atmosphere was quiet, tranquil, romantic and oh-so lovely.

I have many beautiful memories of the things he did for me, such as the surprise birthday party he threw for me on my twenty-fourth birthday. All of our friends gathered to celebrate, and I was so surprised when out of the darkness, they all shouted — Surprise! Then there was the time he left the typewriter I had admired, wrapped in ribbon and waiting for me in my apartment.

I remember one year I had been looking through a Spiegel catalog, just for fun, dog-earring the pages of the outfits I liked. I suppose the catalog was lying around the apartment somewhere and I had forgotten all about it. On my birthday, Victor came in carrying a pile of boxes he couldn't even see over. He put them in front of me and watched excitedly as I opened every single one of the outfits I had admired in the catalog. I was speechless!

I'll never forget the hours we spent together, picking out the perfect diamond and setting for my engagement ring. We wanted it just right. He was so nervous and quiet the night he actually proposed. During dinner at the La Coquina, a restaurant in the Grand Cypress hotel, he asked me to close my eyes as he slid a black velvet box across the table. When I opened it, I looked up at him, his eyes reflected the flickering candlelight, and he shyly asked, "Natalie, will you marry me?" My playful response was, "I'll think about it." I'm sure this was not the response he was hoping all this spellbinding romance would elicit and for a second, he looked a bit perplexed because this was the second time he had proposed. But as that expression faded, I saw that he knew, as did I, that the answer would be yes.

* * *

On the day after Thanksgiving in 1986, we were married after a two-year engagement. The theme of our wedding was "Sharing our Joy", because that's what we wanted - for our friends and family to come and share with us the joy we found in each other.

The first thing Victor said to me as we joined hands on the altar was, "You are beautiful." And he made me feel it. He was so handsome in his gray tux and matching cummerbund. I remember thinking that he seemed so cool and calm in comparison to my wedding jitters. We exchanged the vows we wrote to each other, gave each other rings, and kissed to seal our commitment. I loved our wedding, even though I was so glad when it was over. I was exhausted and ever so anxious to whisk away and get comfortable with my friend, my comforter, my protector, my new husband.

Victor planned our honeymoon in secret, and took care of every detail, including telling me what to bring. He was proud of himself for not leaking any of the surprise, and I was proud of him too because the time in Aruba was magical. We went scuba diving in the clear, blue waters of the Caribbean and played at the Blackjack tables when the sun set. It was special. A souvenir of our honeymoon, a large conch shell with our names painted on it, sat atop the bookcase in our family room.

All too soon, we had to leave the balmy beaches of Aruba and return to real life. Victor back to long nights making busts with the Orange County Sheriff's Departments's Drug Unit, and I to the night shift in the laboratory at Winter Haven

Hospital. Though life was busy, we were happy and content. Those days felt good. They were great.

They were the times that dreams are made of.

After living in a couple of apartments where Victor would work security in exchange for reduced rent rates, he decided to start looking for a home for us to buy. He found a perfect little VA foreclosure house that someone had vacated very quickly, as if they knew we were coming. They even left their food in the refrigerator! We knew it was the house for us when we saw the hot tub built into the lanai and yes, a fireplace in the living room. We were so excited about this house. Together, we spent hours picking out the tile, carpet, and wallpaper designs together, trying out different color combinations to find the one that was just right for our first home.

He worked the evening shift, so I would wait up for him. I looked forward to hearing the key turn in the door when he came in from work. We would spend the evening in the hot tub talking about work, dreams, and each other. We would fall asleep, relaxed and comfortable with life the way it was. Assuming, as is natural, at this stage of life, that it would always follow the same path . . . that nothing would stand in the way of our happiness.

Sometimes I feel foolish.

Had I been duped by a sweet-talking man?

Was I so naive I couldn't see it?

I know love is blind, and I know too often we see only the things we want to see. I suppose I could continue to rationalize. Honestly, I don't believe there was ever a reason to doubt his integrity and the genuineness of his love for me.

I would have to struggle to remember any of these good times as more of his "other life" was revealed to me. But in the beginning, I had nothing but confidence that he would be with me, through sickness and health, for better or worse, for richer or for poorer, in good times and in bad.

CHAPTER 2

Oh, to be a Grandmother

"Grandchildren are the crowning glory of the ages; parents are the pride of their children."

Proverbs 17:6

It had all begun so wonderfully and with so much promise. I always wanted to have a big family. I guess the memories of being an only child bore in me the deep desire for my kids to have lots of brothers and sisters to play with. It was never really a question for me. Victor and I never really talked about it, but he seemed a little more reluctant. He, being the youngest of four children at home and five more from his parents' previous marriages, probably saw the challenges of a large family firsthand, especially for the breadwinner.

He was raised with his three older sisters, and his father worked away from home on the railroad. Victor's father died when Victor was only 13. Betty was the oldest of the sisters, then Nora and the youngest sister, Gail was the closest to him in age by three years. Victor often talked about

Nora taking him to work with her when he was only six years old. She was the one he trusted with money. I never formed a close relationship with his mother or sisters. We all had preconceived notions of each other which started early in the relationship and we never got beyond them. Our lack of a warm relationship seemed okay with Victor, as he spent most of the time with my family. There were times in the early years when I think I tried to form a relationship with his sisters and mother, and I'm sure there were times when they think they tried also. Betty was the sister who always seemed to want to give me a chance and we worked at trying to be sisters-in-laws, but in the end there would prove to be too much history and too many secrets.

Victor and I were surprised and a bit reluctant when I became pregnant in 1988. We were still enjoying the footloose and fancy-free lifestyle of married professionals, and we didn't know how a baby would change all of that. But it didn't take long to get used to the idea. We became very excited about our anticipated addition. I could still remember the first time I felt her move inside me. Victor went to every sonogram and just about every office appointment with me. He was so supportive and right by my side in the delivery room.

We planned on naming our first child Victoria, after her father. The day after she was born by C-section, he walked into the room with a baby-naming book and declared that he liked the name Krystal. I agreed, so a few days later we brought into our home and life, a beautiful brown-eyed, baby girl named Krystal.

She was a colicky baby.

She'd cry and cry, especially in the evenings. Victor would come home and pick her up in his big hands and gently rock her. I remember how comforting it was to watch this big tough man being so gentle with his little baby. At the time, I admired how easily he switched roles from a rough drug cop to a gentle father. On the nights, when he knew I needed a break, he would take over rocking and walking duty. It seemed to be the only thing that soothed the colicky baby. He was so good with her.

Without a doubt, the adjustment came easily. After an extended maternity leave, I started working part-time while my mother, a very proud, first time grandma watched the baby. Victor started working more hours, and took more off-duty jobs to keep our income level the same. We turned in my Toyota Supra and bought a Nissan Maxima, a more family friendly car. I was reluctant to sell that Supra, since it had been my first car. My father and I enjoyed picking it out together, and I remember that he was as excited as I was.

Next, I set my mind on having our next baby. When I brought this up with Victor, he wasn't crazy about the idea. He thought things were good the way they were. But he knew I wanted it so he'd say yes sometimes and then no sometimes, and then yes.

One weekend, he took me to Paradise Island in the Bahamas. There beneath the swaying palm trees, he told me that he wasn't ready for more kids. Neither of us realized that I had already become pregnant, probably the night before he made this announcement. Since I worked in a laboratory, I took a pregnancy test a few weeks after we returned. It was positive. When I called to tell him the news, his reply was, "Well, I hope you're satisfied." I was. It was exactly what I wanted. And I was confident that he would come around.

He did. How could he not when he saw his second beautiful daughter, who joined our family in 1991? We sold our cute little foreclosure home, and when she was 10 days old, we moved to our second home, a four-bedroom, two-bath house, with a pool, and there it was, a fireplace. It was in a nice neighborhood — the perfect house for a perfect family.

As a result, I began working less and less, and Victor worked more and more. It was part of the machismo, the misconception that a man is entitled to do what he wants as long as he "provides" for his family. He figured that he was doing his part to its fullest by bringing home the proverbial bacon. We saw each other a little less, talked a little less. When we did talk, it began to be primarily about the kids. It was our life, and we loved watching them grow and play as they became real little people. We talked about preschools and potty-training, the latest Little Tikes toys and what milestone they accomplished that day. We didn't talk much about our plans for having more children. I knew I was not done having kids and he said that he could be. I didn't really believe him because he adored the kids once they got here. I figured he was just saying that because the girls were so little and life was changing so fast.

Although he never said it, he seemed to miss our footloose lifestyle, whereas I relished in all that we had — the family. I never felt as he did, that we were missing out. People would tease us and say things like, "Don't you all know where babies come from?" or "Maybe someone should buy you a TV." We'd just laugh along with them. When the subject about Victor getting a vasectomy would come up, he would always respond in a bragging, macho tone, that he would get one, but his wife didn't want him to. This was true. I had always heard about an increased risk of prostate cancer in black men and I didn't want to subject my husband and father of my children to any increased health risks, besides, I hadn't made up my mind on limiting our family yet.

In March of 1994, the Lord blessed us with our third little girl. Now we needed another car seat and I pretty much stopped working all together. Victor started to feel more distant, working more and talking less. We babysat for each other. When I did work, my job was flexible enough that I could be scheduled opposite times of his work schedule. This left little couple time.

I also began to feel that Victor somehow resented my not bringing in the same paycheck that I used to when I was working full time. He never said it, but it was something I felt. Although he liked to brag that his wife didn't work, he began to feel the strain of being the sole provider of a growing family. I just seemed to sense more respect when I was more of his equal, financially.

Anyway, putting all this aside, we were grateful not to have to put the kids in daycare, but there was just so little time for the two of us to be together. Hindsight is always 20/20. I can see, that this was not a good recipe for a marriage. Couples need couple time. Time away together makes for better parents and better partners. I never let it cross my mind that he missed the freedom we used to share and was seeking his thrills somewhere else.

Indeed, I was happy in my role as a mother. I always enjoyed being pregnant. I took good care of myself, took my prenatal vitamins, ate well, and stayed away from all the things the doctors said to stay away from.

I loved looking at things in the baby department, waiting to tell Victor all about the newest items. I always saved as much as I could to pass down to each new arrival. Thus, I'd tell myself that we didn't need the latest newfangled stuff because they are really only tiny babies for a few months, but sometimes the new things were just so tempting.

In any case, Victor seemed ambivalent each time he found out that we were pregnant again. I perceived that the early phases of the pregnancies didn't really excite him, and I was always so sick for the first trimester, that it wasn't pleasant for me either. The more pregnancies that we had, the less enthusiasm Victor seemed to muster. He expressed regrets about the relationship he had with his own father. He longed for those father-son memories. But as my tummy got bigger, and the time got closer, he would get more accepting and excited and seemed to forget about his reluctance.

Undeniably, being a mother was a fantasy come true for me. I had looked forward to this since I was a little girl. I dreamed of the big Christmas get-together, when all my children would come home with their spouses and the grand kids. I could see my kids arriving on Christmas Eve and I'd have the tree bursting with packages, all neatly wrapped for my grandchildren. They'd wake me up Christmas morning to open gifts and ignore my insincere complaints about the predawn awakening. Finally, I'd get out of bed to the giggles and excitement that only children can bring to Christmas. Happily, I'd watch with anticipation as they ripped off the ribbons and paper as they opened each gift.

Later in the day, we'd have a big Christmas dinner and the grand kids would play with their new toys and of course, fight over them too. After a couple of days, the kids and grand kids would leave one by one. I knew I would cry as each one would kiss me goodbye and went back to their own life. But, as I shut the door on one Christmas, I would already begin to dream about the next, and what a wonderful, enchanting time it would be.

After the house was quiet, I would sit on the porch in a big ol' rocking chair and reminisce with the husband of my youth, talking about our wonderful family and the joy they brought to our lives. We'd laugh as we talked about which kids were "Just like we used to be at that age."

Even with the doubts that I was starting to have, I thought I had married a man who shared this vision. My biggest dream in life was to be a grandmother. I had always taken it for granted that I would be, and that God had heard this prayer.

CHAPTER 3

A Little Magic Changes the Game

"Riches won't help on the day of judgment, but right living
is a safeguard against death."

Proverbs 11:4

The lack of communication and understanding between us began to wear away not only the foundation of our commitment to each other, but also the foundation of my self-esteem. I began to feel lousy about who I was, and found my only real joy and satisfaction in my children. I was overweight, on a cycle of nursing or pregnant every two years . . . feeling inadequate about my job . . . my husband seemingly happier away from home . . . and I was wishing things were much different from the reality that I was living.

At the same time, I was starting to feel that I could never please my mother. Feeling that I could never please anybody.

Unquestionably, I felt unattractive and devalued. I always had a baby in my uterus or at my breast. I felt so bad about myself that I didn't feel worthy of dressing up or doing my hair. Not only did I not feel worthy, but there wasn't the time. I just didn't have time for it all.

Sometimes my mother or Victor would give me money as a Christmas or birthday gift and tell me to buy something for myself. But I would spend it on the kids - because they were the ones who loved me unconditionally and brought me joy. My mother would shop for me sometimes because she saw that Victor was obviously taking care of himself. Always concerned about how he looked — he never went without a haircut or taking one last look in the mirror.

I had let myself go.

I felt I had no validation or outside encouragement that I was doing a good job as a mother. Victor certainly didn't recognize the work I did or try to convince me that I was a good mother. The world doesn't go out of its way to lift up homemakers, putting much more value in what women do outside of the home. I had girlfriends who helped me feel valuable — but I needed it from my husband as well.

Nonetheless, I always wanted to be a good mother. It was more important to me than any executive position or bank full of money. Perhaps my expectations of myself as a mom were too high. I thought I should be "super mom" and disappointed myself when I was just "Mom."

It took me a long time to realize that just being a good mom was okay, and that taking some time away from my children didn't constitute neglect. I thought to neglect myself, somehow reflected that I was a better mother. Boy was I wrong, this crazy idea only led to burnout and fed into a vicious cycle of over achievement and disappointment. I can't get it right, so I need to do it better . . . but I can't get that right either. I began to undermine myself. I bought into every self defeating thought put in my way.

Meanwhile, I knew that my children needed me, but I increasingly felt that my husband didn't. I felt I had no outlet for these growing negative emotions. I felt like I would burst. I thought there was no one to listen. Somehow I allowed my mother to become the misplaced focus of my growing anger. I knew the relationship with my mother was bruised during this time, but I needed someone to hear me.

Life just didn't seem to make sense anymore. It seemed out of balance. We needed something to come into our lives and help us start to regain our equilibrium.

Change did come in the summer of 1994. It was during this time that Victor was offered a position to work as a security officer with the NBA's Orlando Magic. He was said to have been chosen because they felt he wasn't one to be "star-struck." He would still work for the sheriff's department, but his assignment would be to the Magic. What looked like a good thing came in to further damage our wounded marriage, like a wolf in sheep's clothing.

Victor believed this was the "chance of a lifetime." He would travel with the team to away games as well as be there at many home games and even some practices. Occasionally, he would work as a personal security guard for some of the players when they went to dinner or parties. He would board the Magic Carpet, the team's plane, and fly off into the wide, blue yonder with a plane full of millionaires. It didn't offer a lot of money for the amount of time he would be away from his family, but it came with a lot of perks, a lot of fun, a lot of rubbing shoulders with the big boys, and a lot of exposure to the ladies.

He was so excited. It was contagious. Soon, I too was convinced it was a once-in-a-lifetime, can't pass-it-up opportunity.

He seemed so appreciative of my support of his new endeavor. But, neither of us could see the challenges that it would present to our marriage. I thought this man had his head on straight and was emotionally strong enough to handle the bigger than life temptations that surrounded him. My parents could see what was to come.

When we presented them with the idea, they said, "Don't do it." They advised Victor that what he couldn't pass up was being a father to his children. They wanted him to know that family was the only once-in-a-lifetime opportunity that could never be passed up. They told us that it would be a mistake . . . that he'd regret being away so much . . . the Magic job would zap the vitality out of our already strained family life . . . And the damage to the household would be enormous. The minimal benefits weren't worth the immeasurable risks.

We didn't want to hear it. We were like teenagers getting our first set of wheels. No matter how many warnings of driving slow and wearing seat belts we got, we were hell bent on pushing the limits of our new found freedom, and we jumped into that car together and headed straight for a tragic collision.

I was looking for my parent's approval, but instead they gave advice. They were only trying to help, but I felt if they were not supporting my husband then they were not supporting me. I was blindly following the unhealthy desires of my husband. We couldn't hear good, old-fashioned common sense.

Couldn't my parents see this was the saving grace for my marriage and not the doom and gloom they predicted? Why couldn't they see the other side? Why did they have to be so practical?

The Magic job would prove to be a mistake endorsed by the devil himself.

My parents were right.

Victor was never home. We seldom talked. He went to this city and that city. I'd ask him to stop traveling so much, as did my parents. He once told my father, "Other women can run a household alone, why can't Natalie?" My father tried to help, but the position with the Magic watered the seeds of discontentment that were already sprouting in

Victor. I saw his values change. But did they really, or had I seen signs of this before? Were they resurfacing with so much more to feed them?

I began to wonder why I couldn't satisfy my husband's need to roam . . . love . . . and romance me again. The Magic took my magic away and viciously fed into my self doubt. It was chipping away at what was left of my self-esteem and taking away the person that I had been. When my friends talked about the person they knew years before, I could barely remember who she was. Was that really me? You really remember me as taking good care of myself? Was I really a good mother? Who was this person, where did she go? What happened to her, and most important, how could I get her back?

Once the kids and I were looking through my college yearbook. As we were reading through the autographs again, one word was mentioned more than any other — potential. My potential. How did I lose sight of that? Why did I allow myself to feel that I was so undeserving of my dream - a family? Many people had seen enough possibilities in me to write about them. Somehow, somewhere, I lost sight of my own potential.

As time would have it, by the summer of 1996, I was well into my fourth pregnancy with our first son, who was born in October of that year. It was all such a whirlwind. Baby made three, four, five and six within seven short years. We began growing in different directions. There was no more couple-time or couple-thought. When little Vic was only three weeks old, Victor took off to Japan, leaving his sister Betty to help me with three young kids and a newborn. We began living a life apart while living together as this big, God-given, growing family.

Although it wasn't always obvious where his family fit into his list of priorities at the time, I never questioned whether or not Victor loved the kids. One of our favorite short trips was to take them to K-Mart to ride the quarter operated riding toys. Sometimes I'd take them, but when Victor did, you would have thought he was taking them to Disney World with how excited he'd get about these little trips. Once he came back telling me how disgusted he was that some teenagers were playing around with these rides that his kids enjoyed. He never said a word to them, but his presence and stern glares were enough to make them move along.

As the children got older and involved at school, he was there as much as many dads. I was there too, volunteering at centers or doing Math Superstars as much as our shifting schedules would allow. From all outward appearances, he was a great dad. He loved to go on the school field trips.

We went our separate ways with our own ideas and goals. Rarely did we come to a firm agreement about anything. He was uncomfortable expressing his feelings, and I, so overwhelmed with being a mother and my own broken self image, just didn't have time or know how to play psychologist to draw him out. It takes effort and time from both partners to communicate. By the time I tried to make more of an effort with him, by the time I started to suggest we spend more time together, set goals together, and all that . . . he didn't think it was necessary. He believed he had it all figured out. I felt we were too far gone.

Blinded by love, I couldn't see it. If he could not find contentment at home, he would seek it elsewhere. Where was my head? Why was I determined to be so blind, to have such undying loyalty in light of what was right in my face?

How could a marriage which started out with so much promise, now be so lonesome?

When I tried to breech the subject of spending more time together . . . about finding someone to replace him for some of the road trips and being home more, he would turn and walk out the door leaving me all alone with the children and my bruised self-esteem. To watch him turn away from me, walk down the hall and out the door was emotionally devastating, to put it mildly. I destroyed me inside.

When he came home a couple of days later, I would act out. My frustration level was at an all time high. I would throw things and shout in an effort to be heard. I wasn't. I just wanted my friend, my protector, my husband back. I tried desperately to get him to hear my pain. I was hurting inside and he never saw it, or didn't care.

Lonesome began to be the word of choice.

Still, I kept the card that he gave me the first time he went on a road trip with the team. It was one of those that just melts a wife's heart. It spoke of appreciation, love, honor, and understanding. It was one of the sweetest cards ever. It was priceless. I would read it over and over trying to find something to hang on to. He would leave many notes, cards, flowers and call continuously during the first several months of trips.

In six short months, all gestures dwindled to little of nothing. I could see the change in his beautiful brown eyes. The same eyes that had looked so lovingly across the table at me when he proposed. He talked about the parties he attended, the houses he visited, the cars he rode in, and the big name players he was socializing with.

Consequently, I was convinced that the job with the Magic took a small town boy who liked the "simple things," and threw him into a big pot, boiling with big cities, glamour, glitz, money, and an awesome gig where he could hang out with some of the biggest names in basketball and the entertainment world.

I wasn't the only one who saw it. My parents said they would never forget those days - the detachment they began to see. They used to tell me that he was too busy to raise a family, and they were terribly bothered by his moodiness. I can only imagine what he was exposed to when he was around the players. Shaq, Penny, Brian, Darrell, Nick and

Horace - not that any of these were bad guys, but their lifestyle and deep pockets of money were more than this small-town boy with glitter in his eyes could take. I could see, that the warm glow of family in his eyes had been replaced by the Magic.

Victor told me that once when he boarded the team's plane, one of the players looked up and tugged at the end of his too short coat's sleeve and said, "Hmm, a little African boy." The whole plane burst with laughter and Victor tried to make the best of it. When he told me about it, I could tell that deep down, it injured his ego very badly. I believe even then he was thinking, "You might laugh at me now, but watch me later."

Penny, whom Victor seemed to have formed an especially close relationship to, was young, rich, single, and appeared to be making quite an impression on Victor. He would just look around Penny's house in awe and say to me, "We'll live like this one day." I thought, "Right." I really had no need to live that way. Yeah, the house was okay, but it wasn't for plain, everyday people like us, which I guess was part of the problem. Victor didn't want to be, nor did he see himself as a plain, everyday person - he wanted to be a real part of his new found peer group - whatever they did.

I guess it's why the Bible set aside one of its Ten Commandments to address coveting what your neighbor has. Pining over things that are so out of reach leads only to discontentment. Victor no longer saw his wife, family and the more than adequate possessions we had as enough. He wanted more. More money . . . more possessions . . . more prestige . . . and more excitement than his continually pregnant or nursing wife could provide.

He wanted more, not something else. He wanted his family and his fun. He wanted his proverbial cake and a silver spoon to eat it with. And he got it, for a while at least. I later found out that he had other women to feed his need for more of everything. I suppose, if I had really thought about it, I could have figured it out. There had been enough signs. People told me I didn't want to know, and maybe I didn't. I just never believed Victor, that lovely romantic man I married would ever stoop that low. I thought he was better than that. I held onto the good days, to the nights in the hot tub and the man who was so gentle with his newborns.

I needed to believe in him.

I needed us back where we used to be. Once I called the general manager of the Magic to encourage him to intervene and make Victor's schedule more family friendly. Victor was furious about this. I wanted to schedule the road trips that he was expected to take so that it would allow more time at home. I also wanted to get a better idea of how much money he was being paid. I believe the GM felt like he was in the middle of something that Victor and I should have worked through. He was right about that, but if I felt the need to call, then obviously I wasn't getting the answers I needed at home. The Magic was a family oriented organization and sensitive to family concerns. The next season, Victor didn't travel nearly as much with the team and supposedly it was because of my phone call to the general manager.

Would my phone call help my home life? Only time would tell.

CHAPTER 4

Can I Buy This for Free?

" . . . an adulterous person can satisfy their sexual appetite,
shrug their shoulders, and then say,
what's wrong with that?"

Proverbs 30:20

I had endured years of the growing distance, culminating
with Victor's job with the Orlando Magic. We had just
sold our second house and temporarily moved into a nice
townhouse while we looked for our next home. Things
were strained between Victor and me during this time and I
really didn't know if we would ever move into a third house
together as a married couple.

Victor was unpredictable, especially at night. Where
was he? Why didn't I insist on some accountability? He
always had a believable excuse for his absence. He covered
his bases well, telling others how many off-duty jobs he had
to work. He even gave his mother information to help validate his whereabouts. When I talked to her, she would tell
me how Victor worked off duty jobs from morning 'til

night. I'd tell myself that he surely wouldn't lie to his mother. I allowed myself to believe all that he said.

Distant is not an accurate word to describe our relationship. Indifferent was more like it. I was tired of being taken for granted. I had my fill of it. This was going to be the night to take my stand and he was going to know that I wasn't taking any more of his abuse.

I was putting him out.

Victor's sister owned a funeral home. At one o'clock in the morning on a cool, crisp night in early 1998, while Victor was sleeping, I took every piece of his clothing to the funeral home where his sister and mother lived and left them there. I took them one by one out of the back of my van and laid them under the car porch alongside a long white hearse that carried dead bodies. Perhaps that night symbolized the death of my marriage too.

As soon as Victor's mother and sister awoke the next morning and saw his clothes lying outside, they were shocked, and mad. They indignantly asked, "What type of person would do something like that?" Never once asking the more important question, "What had Victor done to make her do something like that?" His sister didn't need to ask, she knew. It later became very clear to me that they would never see any wrong in Victor's actions. He never erred in their eyes and his sister would cover for him in any situation. He had no accountability to anyone, especially to me.

I suppose putting the clothing out wasn't the most prudent thing to do. What I really wanted to throw out was Victor's indifference and irresponsibility. I was just sick of it. I was tired of the loneliness. We tried some counseling, and I had done everything I knew of to get things right between us. We saw our counselor once or twice a week for several months. It was expensive, but Victor was always very willing and able to pay it. Surely we would find new love. I was honest about my feelings and the things that troubled me. Victor kept every appointment and participated, but it didn't seem to be moving us closer to living together again.

Looking back on these sessions, I can see that this counseling was all about me changing and not Victor. Counseling can only work if there is complete honesty and you both are working toward the same goal. My total desire was to fix this. Reflecting back, the sessions were filled with deceptions and lies on Victor's part because when he left our sessions, he was returning to the home of another woman. The sessions were a waste of time and money, mostly his, or as some people have hinted, hers.

My parents tried one last time to talk to Victor, but if it didn't go along with his plan, he didn't want to hear it. By now, they were done trying to talk to him. They felt they had said all they could say and weren't willing to try anymore. Looking back, I knew they saw things that I couldn't yet see.

By putting the clothes out, I figured Victor would see that I had reached my limit. I believed he would make a choice, the right choice, and be responsible enough to come home. Perhaps he'd have a big, fat hand of reality slap him across the face and he'd come to his senses. It didn't work. He didn't argue the separation. Later he told me that I would never know what it felt like to be put out and what it did to him.

Again, it was all about him.

Putting him out wasn't my mistake, that might have been the strong statement that I needed to make. Backing down and seeming sorry about it was the mistake I made. If I was strong enough to do it, then I should have been strong enough to stand by it, especially if there was no change in actions on his part. Sometimes you have to truly let something go in order to see if it was meant to be. I couldn't yet do this. I feared really losing him.

How can you lose something that is already lost?

Some time later, after I found out about it, I asked him

why he lived with this woman since he so adamantly stated, "I cared nothing about her." His answer, "It was more convenient, I guess." This woman was rumored to have inherited a lot of money, which she spent on Victor. Victor hadn't learned yet that nothing comes free. Everything has a price.

Anyway, the kids and I remained in the townhouse. Victor still payed all the bills and supported us financially. He still maintained the philosophy of not wanting his wife to work. He came by in the mornings to take the kids to school. He would visit them regularly and help me out when I needed to service a vending route that I owned at the time. I had purchased this route with the intent of earning money while I stayed available for the kids. I owned seven drink and snack machines which could earn some easy money and only needed to be serviced about two days a week. Sometimes he went to help me with the machines, although, I think he really went to spy on a guy whom he accused me of having a relationship with. Victor expressed extreme anger about the thought of me sleeping with someone else. He directly accused me of it.

As I recall now, the anger in his eyes was frightening, almost animalistic. It was not true, but this was a sign of his own infidelity that I didn't recognize. Victor was judging me by his standards.

He was "projecting" on me, things that were true about him. As I have learned, projection is a well known psychoanalytic theory. It's a psychological defense. Sometimes people won't allow themselves to face what is true about them. They can't bear to get in touch with their own feelings especially if they are very deep and painful. Victor was painting his feelings on me. That made it easier to criticize and attack things which were really his own actions.

I admit, the attention of the other guy was flattering, and I enjoyed his wit. Victor was so serious and moody, and this man made me laugh. I really needed to laugh. For the few minutes that I spoke with him on my vending trips, I began to enjoy the conversation. I think he was interested in something more, but he knew I was married. What is more important, I knew I was married, and that's all there was to that. Victor over and over threatened to go and confront him. The thought amused me because this guy was pretty big and street tough. I urged him to go ahead. I felt Victor was barking up the wrong tree with this guy and just might get his bell rung if he went. He never did.

I later found out that it was so easy for Victor to come by the townhouse because he and this woman lived five minutes down the street. I knew that he didn't live far because he quickly got to the townhouse if we paged him. I just wasn't sure in which direction. He always told us that he lived with his sister, who also lived five minutes down the street, so there was a part of me that still wanted to believe him. His accomplice in the charade was his sister Gail. She knew where he lived and what he was doing. I can only guess that his sister must have thought all this was okay since I put her brother out, and since I was "the sister-in-law everyone loved to hate," so I was told.

Gail and this woman were friends until the woman accused her brother of rape, stalking, and domestic violence. Victor asked his sister to intervene with the woman when he was scared these charges might cause some embarrassment. She did. The proof of this was Gail's business card that she left on the woman's fence with a hand written note to "call me."

Obviously, I knew that Victor was an attractive man and drew the attention of other women while we were separated. I felt there was nothing I could have done about it, and didn't feel strong enough to try.

A man who would act like this was already lost to me, but more importantly to himself.

Would a confrontation have helped? One of my good

friends confronted him about having an affair. He said, "I'm not having an affair, I'm not that kind of man." He told her that when we got back together, she would be the first casualty. She wasn't. With arrogance and confidence he returned to the other woman's bed each night. I accepted the promises and assurances, not wanting to see anything else.

I was in my spiritual desert - alone and lonely. I was looking for something. I knew a meaningful element was missing from our lives. Something that we so badly needed. Nothing else helped, nothing else seemed to make a difference. How long would I allow myself to wander before I sought real strength - in God?

* * *

Victor had been reluctant to tell the kids about the separation and I couldn't really understand why. It was real, why not tell them the truth? He didn't want to, so I did, to help them understand why Dad wasn't living with us. He said very little. He saw their hurt and heard them cry, but still did nothing. He just sat there as if all this was happening to someone else. Sex, money, cars and convenience were more luring than the cries of his children.

The good thing, the best thing that happened during this time was that I began to talk to God. Not only did I talk with Him, many times in the loneliness of my bedroom, I wept to Him. He became very real in my life for the first time in many years. In my desperation we developed a strong, intimate relationship. I began to learn more about and spend time with Him. He became my rock, my strength, my Man.

I never could have imagined just how important that relationship was going to be to me in the future. Looking back, I can see that this was a preparation time. A training time when God said, "Natalie, there will come a time when you are not going to be able to rely on any man for anything,

so you'd better just start learning right now, to rely on me."
And I did.

During this time, I tried to get Victor to attend church. I taught Sunday school and enjoyed it. I wanted my whole family to join in the excitement and fulfillment that I found in joining a church and having a relationship with Jesus. Whenever I invited Victor to come to Bible study, church, or a seminar for married couples, he would come. One Sunday, when he was attending church with us, my pastor did an altar call and told us to turn to the person next to you and say, "I'll go with you." I thought about the saying, "The family that prays together, stays together." I wanted badly for Victor to join his wife and children in worship, so I turned to him and extended the invitation by saying, "Victor, I'll go with you." He said no. I left it at that.

I accepted his refusal and continued to teach Sunday school and worship while he sometimes came over to keep the kids on Sunday morning, if I needed him to. He was making his choice, and I was making mine. It felt right.

Regardless, I still kept on praying that he'd return, and slowly I began to see small signs that it might happen. We even spent a couple of weekends together to start repairing our relationship. I just kept on praying.

Victor was gone for a full year. When the townhouse lease was up, the kids and I moved from the townhouse, into a smaller apartment. We fell into our disjointed family routine.

I really felt during this time that I had some chronic illness. My insides were in a perpetual knot. I had constant heart palpitations and continuous fatigue from the stress of it all. I saw a cardiologist who ordered a stress test and said that I was fine. So, since my tests were all normal, I put it out of my mind and just accepted that all my symptoms were due to my current stressful circumstances. I didn't think about it much anymore. I still didn't feel fine though, and I wished that for a moment, just a moment, that I could get off this emotional and physical roller coaster.

How could someone who was once your friend, comforter and confidant, bring such pain?

* * *

On New Year's Day 1999, the kids and I had gone out. When we returned to the small apartment, we found Victor mopping the kitchen floor. I thanked him for it and said that I would finish so he could visit with the kids. He didn't say anything, he just kept mopping. I offered a couple of times, but he kept mopping. I finally knew that he was back. He brought his things from his car, saying he wanted to come home. Of course I let him come. He said he belonged here with us. I had waited a year for this. As I welcomed him back into our home he told me, "The one thing you can't do is ask me where I've been staying for the past year."

I was so happy to have him home that I agreed, and was willing to put all that behind us.

It's a sad fact, but his woman fed his desire to live the "big-life." His family and some of his co-workers knew of his adultery. They helped him hide it, without regard for his family. Victor claimed he left the woman because he wanted to come home to us. The woman claimed it was because she wanted to get on with her life. I'm sure the truth was somewhere in the middle. All of this I did not find out about until later.

I was his wife. Why didn't I ask the questions and insist on the answers I deserved? Why was I willing to settle for so little? Was it because I still was not ready for those very answers that might have forced me into a place that I was not prepared for? Was it because I no longer felt valuable enough to be loved?

* * *

That Valentine's Day, in the parking lot of the O-rena (Orlando arena), before going into a Magic game, I gave him a new, shiny gold wedding band. He responded with enthusiasm. He put it on immediately and kissed me. I took this as a sign that he was ready to commit again. That he had come back to his senses and we were officially going to be a family again.

But a family can't grow in a shadow of secrets. Eventually, everything has to come into the light.

CHAPTER 5

And Walls Came Tumbling Down

> ". . . The body is not for immorality, but for the Lord, and the Lord is for the body."
>
> I Corinthians 6:13

Victor had been a golden boy, a hero, a star. He made strides in his career that no other African-American man had ever done, being appointed in 1989 to be the aide to Sheriff Walt Gallagher, a respected position in the Orange County Sheriff's Department.

Reflecting back, although I didn't know, it was during this time that rumors of his infidelities and the blurring of the lines between right and wrong began to emerge within the sheriff's department. So I learned, it was then that the gossip mill was saying he had women meet him at his off duty jobs and in hotel rooms which he had access to by virtue of his position.

Nonetheless, little by little a man of great promise walked deeper into darkness until, eventually, there was no way out.

He had begun his descent on what the Federal Bureau of Investigation (F.B.I.) agents called the "slippery slope" theory. First you get by with little things, then you keep sliding down that slope as you start to believe you can get by with more and more. Eventually, you are caught on a slope where the sliding gets faster and faster and you can't grab anything to stop your descent - you either get caught or killed.

As one of my friends observed, "If Victor got by with A, he'd do B, and if he got by with B, he'd do D, and if he got by with D, he'd go all the way to X, Y, and Z."

Nevertheless, everything he did was with competence that quickly made him the "go-to-guy" in the sheriff's department. He had administrative abilities, and a charisma that gave people a sense of confidence. It was rumored that one day he would be elected the first African-American sheriff in Orange County history. Some of his "business associates" even told him that when he ran for sheriff, they would contribute to his campaign. Some of these "business associates" turned out to be F.B.I. informants.

Victor had spent seven years in the undercover drug unit, and most of these years, he was "in charge." Anyone can tell you that seven years is a long haul in a covert line of duty. There is something about being involved in that innately deceptive work that begins to whittle away at a man's character. There's only so much a human being can resist without the strength of a more powerful being. When you master the art of deception and lying, they can creep into your soul like air into your lungs.

Deception is a craft that becomes easier when practiced daily. Satan thirsts for more and more of you until you are totally consumed. He wants your soul and all that your life has to offer.

The undercover unit took on a street name, "the Duke Boys," after a popular 80's hit television show, "The Dukes of Hazzard." The "Duke Boys" had a reputation around

Orange County of being tough, efficient, and made some of the biggest drug busts in the county. They printed a poster with the unit dressed in their hoods and bulletproof vests. They projected an image of invincibility. Their posters were displayed in offices around town.

Victor had the reputation of being "One of the best undercover drug officers the sheriff's office ever had." I was told that he could sit with any drug dealer and sell him anything. He could talk a dog off of a meat wagon if that's what Victor wanted - he could speak the language of the streets.

He was not from the streets, but he became the streets. I always suspected that his extended assignment in the drug unit had a negative impact on the core of whom he was. It goes back to the old saying, "If you lie down with dogs, you're going to get fleas."

Thinking back on the "Duke Boy" days, I can't really put my finger on the exact changes I saw taking place, but I knew that he should have left the unit sooner. I had begun to see hints of a coldness creeping into his personality that I had never seen before. There were the nights out with the "boys," and I thought little of this because I knew all of them and thought they were just hanging out after work. I later learned that there were nights out with the "girls" too.

After his time in the drug unit, he was assigned to several different departments, until he was eventually reassigned to work at the sheriff's department's boot camp for troubled boys. At the camp, his administrative and leadership skills took on a new face. He was out in public, going to meetings and being appointed to committees. He was instrumental in getting the boot camp up and running smoothly in a short amount of time. It was during this time that although he didn't know it, a sheriff's office task force began to look at him closely for more than his administrative abilities, and I first began to know of troubles at work.

Equally, one of his co-workers at the boot camp was

another African-American officer who had been a good friend to the family. Ken was a wise and caring man who believed in Victor's abilities, but also saw his weaknesses. He was aware of many of the problems Victor began to have while working at the camp. He told me of conversations they had in the parking lot after work.

His friend tried to warn him against making the same mistakes he himself had made in his younger years. Victor wouldn't listen and thought he had the answers to it all. When Ken described this attitude, I could believe it because I had seen it all too often. He gravitated toward people who overlooked or condoned his infidelities and gray areas of right and wrong. There were enough of those supporters who gave Victor a false sense of security.

Ken describes what happened to Victor during this time as a kid in a candy shop, eating with reckless abandon, having no warnings of calories or cavities. Ken also describes one other problem that was emerging bigger than life within Victor, his battle with the "lust demon."

According to Ken, the "lust demon" was a problem that Victor didn't handle very well, he didn't want to. He liked the feeling of "walking into a room and heads turning - especially the ladies." With each turn his own head grew. Lots of people had seen "the lady's man" in positions of impropriety, but none had the heart to tell me.

Victor was beginning to spiral out of control, feeling indestructible, behaving recklessly, and hanging around with people who said not a word to him. No one had any idea or was willing to guess where he might be heading, no one except the investigators who had begun to watch him day and night.

Some time later, I ran into an old friend, who worked for the sheriff's department also. Our families had known each other for years. He told me that months before, he ran into him and said, "Man, I hear they're watching you. I don't know what for, but whatever you're doing, you'd better stop." This friend said he was, "Sure Victor was up to his old tricks again and messing with some woman." Victor's reply was, "Don't worry about it man, this is Thomas, I got it, I got it," as he patted his chest.

A perfect storm was brewing in his soul. His time in the drug unit, his promotions, and the exposure to the Magic were sowing the seeds of a person who thought he was "above the law" and entitled to do whatever he wanted.

As I reflect on what I have learned of these times, I really thank God that He blinded me to Victor's adulterous and emerging criminal life. I wouldn't have handled it as well then, and I'm sure God knew that. Emotionally it would have been torment, but moreover, spiritually I was unprepared to hear and deal with the tortuous feelings that adultery, betrayal, and broken vows would do to me and my family. I couldn't face what I would have perceived to be my failure, head on.

As our family life disintegrated, little by little things caught up with Victor at work. He began to be disciplined for abuse of authority. He even had to undergo some counseling within the department in 1998. In 1999, the woman he had lived with pressed charges against him for domestic violence, sexual battery, and stalking. The charges were not sustained. Victor was very concerned that I not hear about all this, and I didn't at the time.

I didn't know much about his discipline at work either. He could easily hide this from me and he did. Looking back, while serving his suspensions, there was always a reason why he was in plain clothes for a couple of days, either he would say he was going to the range, or going to some of his committee meetings. I'm sure with what I know now, much of this time also included time for his serial affairs.

All the same, in September 2000, a month after our fifth child was born, he was penalized 10 hours of pay for once again, usurping authority. October brought about another incident when he involved himself in a traffic call in Winter Park that involved Magic player Horace Grant's body guard. Winter Park is not in the sheriff's department's range of authority, and he should not have been involved in this matter at all. The Winter Park officer involved was said to have felt intimidated by the captain from another agency. Captain Victor Thomas.

After complaints and more investigations, he was penalized 120 hours of pay, and put on a 1-year probationary status. He filed appeals, which were all denied. This was the first time he began to realize that he was not totally immune to punishment. I'm sure he was amazed that his eloquent letters of appeal did not sway the committee.

He appeared woeful, almost sorrowful. He seemed to not understand how this could happen to him. He talked to me about his disappointment — it became a daily conversation. I really felt that we were sharing, and talking again. It appeared as if he needed me again. I believed the pitiful sadness in his face.

The irony of it was, the sheriff's department was ready to fire Victor for his actions. They were told not to, because by now, the F.B.I. was involved in the investigation and they needed to allow it to continue.

Victor made one last desperate attempt to escape punishment when he went to an old friend's house, Malone Stewart who was then the second in charge, the undersheriff. He wanted Malone to hear his plea and ask for help. I encouraged him to go and visit with his old friend. Surely, Victor thought, Malone could help him and get him out of this mess. Victor kept saying to me, "Won't anybody see this thing for what it really is?" He was confident that Malone could see all this and straighten it out. I thought so too. No doubt, there had to be a rock that Malone could turn over for a friend. Malone himself even said that he and

Victor were, "like brothers." Our relationships were close enough that Victor even thought of asking him to be his best man in our wedding.

We were wrong. Malone told Victor that he had put himself in a position where he couldn't help him. Victor couldn't understand this and was visibly hurt. He felt betrayed, almost in tears. I believe that the relationship with Malone was the one that Victor valued the most in the world. They had met when Victor was an F.T.O. We had always been there for Malone and his family even in times of their sensitive family situations. Little did he know, little did many people know except those in positions of authority, that there were much deeper concerns surrounding Victor. Malone knew this.

Also in September of 2000, an undercover investigation had begun tracking a string of illegal activities much more serious than Victor sticking his nose where it did not belong. These activities began to be noted by the authorities, activities that dated as far back as that magic year . . . 1994, the year he started working for the Magic.

When a federal prisoner who had been arrested for possession of three kilograms of cocaine wanted to bargain with the charges against him, he offered, "I know a cop who is dirty." The prisoner informed F.B.I. special agents that he had provided Victor with two vehicles at greatly reduced prices. The cars were in exchange for assistance in protecting an illicit car dealing business and providing law enforcement intervention on his behalf if needed. Research into the Florida Department of Motor Vehicles records uncovered the truth to this man's claims, a 1969 Pontiac GTO was received by Victor in 1994.

There was not much contact between the two men until Victor initiated contact in July 1999, claiming his need for another vehicle. Once again, a deal was made wherein Victor would provide protection and assistance in exchange for a 1994 GMC Sonoma at a greatly reduced price. Subsequently, Victor provided assistance on two separate occasions, protecting this man and his uncle from arrest.

I knew about these cars and even drove some of them, but had no idea they were being obtained by illegal means. Victor said that he had a friend whom he was buying the cars from. Always, if he could find a good deal, a connection on anything, he'd take it.

Upon hearing these details, an operation was set up in October of 2000, with the assistance of a former member of the group running the illicit car dealership. The informant provided taped phone conversations and information to task force agents regarding the ever-increasing criminal activity of Captain Victor Thomas.

His slippery slope allowed no firm footing now and he was slipping at mach speed into icy treacherous waters. On surveillance tape, Victor was recorded as saying to a confidential witness, "Yeah, you do anything in Orlando. You check with me first." Sad. Sad. This was my husband and father of my five children — the self-appointed "prince of the city."

Victor Thomas had risen through the ranks of the sheriff's department all the way from a young officer whom they criticized about the way he wrote his reports, to a captain. He had been given privileges, appointed to the governor's committees, and sat on boards with some of the leading political figures in Orange County. He was one of the boys and he thought this put him above the long arm of the law. At some point in his career, he decided to use all of his God-given talents for his own self-serving purposes, rather than for the good of the citizens of Orange County, those who looked up to him, the people who trusted him, and a family who needed him.

Doctor Jekyll and Mister Hyde, but in a sense, worse. Doctor Jekyll was evil, and sinister, but he didn't have five pairs of innocent, young eyes looking to him as an example of a man, a father and a husband.

This was a man who switched his personalities on and off depending on the door he was walking in. He could compartmentalize and play the role demanded by his audience. If he needed to play the role of the community servant, he could do that. If he needed to don the hat of the adulterer who could fulfill a woman's every desire, he'd play that. If he needed to play the notorious cop who could provide protection for a price, he could do that. And if he needed to play the dutiful father and husband, that was no problem either.

Most people didn't see the problem because Victor was a master of disguises. He didn't change his clothing or put on make-up to deceive others. His methods were more calculating. He changed his words, reactions and demeanor to match his audience. This kind of behavior in itself is disturbing and warrants some type of professional intervention. There would be no intervention, no counseling.

He was out of control.

Have you ever watched a toddler at the beach? They run toward the lapping waves, first daring only to get their feet on wet sand. Then, they let the water touch their toes before they run squealing back to their ever-cautious mother. Emboldened, they get their knees wet, and then their diaper is a little soggier than before. Mother says, "Be careful, don't go in too deep." They run down to the water's edge again and come back with a wet belly. "Careful," says Mom, now following close behind. Soon the brave little explorer gets used to the depth of the water and he ventures a little farther and gets splashed in the face, swallowing a mouthful of nasty salt water, before he falls down on his butt. His laughing mother picks up the sputtering little guy. He's startled and scared and finally realizes that he should have listened to his mother's warnings.

I suppose Victor didn't have anyone to give his life

direction. No inner voice called to him and definitely no outer voice that he would listen to. When you venture into waters that are too deep and you don't want to be stopped, you surround yourself with people who say, "You go boy," or "I just want you to be happy." Any of that is permission enough for a personality being consumed by the devil to delve right into deep, dark waters that are too murky to see the bottom.

A man that prideful needed a strong male mentor to get in his face and tell him what a dead end road he was on and what he was throwing away. As a good friend of mine once said, "He needed five or six strong men about my size (this friend is 6'4" and 300 pounds), to take him to a shed out behind the church and give him a good behind whipping."

Victor had no limits, in any aspects of his life. I should have seen it. I, who was supposed to be closest to him should have seen it. And I did. To an extent. I knew that there was something disturbing about him, something sinister that I couldn't quite pinpoint, but I had no idea how slippery was his slope. Our conversations were shallow. Our deepest conversations occurred when he was scared, but even then he told the story from one perspective - Victor's.

In February of 2001, I asked him to sit and talk with me. He did. We talked about many things, but now I recall saying, "The only difference between you and the people you arrest, is a badge." God had given me the strength and discernment to confront him. Victor turned and looked me straight in the eye and didn't say a word. It was as if he was saying, "You have no idea." Before, I had felt it, but on that day I knew there was something creepy, cold, and eery that had taken control of the man I had known.

It was too late. He was deeply involved in criminal activity. He could have been arrested at any point. The task force, his superiors, and other officers knew that "personality," as they referred to him, would go even deeper into the abyss. They wanted to see it.

He was spending many of his work hours at one of his adulteress' home, which is one reason they started the internal investigation that led to some of the other investigations. The sheriff's department wanted to see if the county taxes were paying him to protect the citizens of Orange County, or to satisfy his adulterous appetite.

Victor was first asked by the informants to check out warehouse space that would be used to store counterfeit merchandise. After completing this task, he was asked if he would like another vehicle. He said he would like a Suburban, Durango, or Tahoe. It was agreed upon that he would receive a Suburban after he drove the vehicle three or four times down to Dade County to transport counterfeit goods.

He was observed driving the vehicle on several occasions and recorded checking out the Suburban that had been purchased by the Orange County Sheriff's Department at an auction. The vehicle was filled with hundreds of thousands of dollars of counterfeit merchandise such as purses, Rolex watches, clothing, sunglasses, computer software and pens. It was ironic that he parked this illegal vehicle in the parking lot of the sheriff's department's offices.

He ran several shipments to south Florida over a period of months. The water was well over his head with no chance to catch a breath.

On January 19 of 2001, Victor was recorded as saying about a confidential witness at a rest stop on the turnpike, "if he —— me, I'll go down there and rid his whole family, I said if he —— me, I'll go down there and rid him of his whole ——— family." The CW (confidential witness) even though a toughened con man himself was said to have been afraid. He said that he had looked into Victor Thomas' eyes and saw that he had no heart. Perhaps Victor suspected that someone was watching him, perhaps he was just "puffing," but according to the F.B.I., this CW was scared.

In February of 2001, he agreed to take his transporting a step further. He was promised $1000 per kilogram to transport 18 kilograms of cocaine. Whatever his motive of making a threat against someone's family, the task force could not allow any physical harm to come to anyone. So they agreed to end the operation and arrest Victor for trafficking in counterfeit merchandise and attempting to possess with intent to distribute cocaine hydrochloride.

I did not know the man who used the "f word" frequently. I could count the times on one hand, in all the years I had known him, that I heard him use profanity. Even in anger, he did not speak that way, or use foul language around me. We didn't use profanity in our home. That was part of the other persona, the one that was so caught up in pleasing himself that nothing else seemed to matter except his own satisfaction.

There was a recorded conversation about Victor, between two CW's as they waited in an area Chili's restaurant for Victor's arrival. From this conversation, even other criminals thought Victor was foolish for throwing away so much.

> " ...Big man, big job. Lot of, Lot of respect, lot of trust, stupid. Stupid. Really stupid. Man if you give me this job tomorrow. Example, F.B.I., DEA, anything like this, man it's no way. There's no way. I don't really (inaudible few words). You know what I mean? Even if I know I can get away with it, you know what I mean? No way. Your life is set, you're done. You're, you're, you're OK. You're perfect, your family is taken care of, you're taken care of. You know, you know you have a lot of people to back you up."

The conversation between the two informants continues,

"I don't believe it. You know what, he deserves it. You know why he deserves it, because he is stupid. He is really stupid. He is making more than $100,000 a year, you know? More than $10,000 a month plus benefits, this, that, traveling. Stupid. Stupid. No, I feel bad for the kids because the kids, you know and it's like they grow up now, they say that their father is, you know . . . "

What drives a man to be so selfish, so consumed with himself that little else matters and especially when there are five children at home, depending on him to be that father that he signed up to be? Unfortunately men commit crimes and they have affairs, but how many men let everything go for this kind of destruction?

I think back to the question that my young daughter asked me, "Why didn't Dad think about his family?"

CHAPTER 6

Come Straight Home

"Such is the fate of all who are greedy for gain. It ends up
robbing them of life."

Proverbs 1:19

One life ended and another began on that March afternoon in 2001.

Victor Thomas was arrested.

It's hard to understand the chain of events that led to my
husband's face being the lead story on the evening news and
on the front page of the newspaper for weeks. How could he
have led a life that got him locked-up, sent to prison —
away from his wife, his kids, his life?

Victor himself is the only one who can really say. The
best I can do is simply look back and put some of the shattered pieces together. Sort of like putting a jigsaw puzzle
together without the picture on the box.

To make the arrest, the F.B.I. and sheriff's department's
task force staged a mock captain's meeting. Victor had been
at home all day keeping our four-year-old son and six-
month-old baby girl while I attended a PTF meeting (Parent

Teacher Fellowship), where I served as the chaplain.

His mood had been solemn and quiet all day. He had been extremely humble toward me, responding with a quiet, "Okay, Natalie," whenever I made a suggestion or comment. He sat in our front yard for a long time under the oak tree, gently holding our baby daughter as she slept. I remember he looked as though he had the weight of the world on his shoulders, and his eyes were full of sadness. I remember not feeling sorry for him at this time. For some unexplainable reason, I didn't buy into it on this day. I believe this was intervention of the Holy Spirit. After months of moodiness, distance and whining, I just wasn't buying the self-pity. Gnawing at my spirit was the feeling that whatever it was, Victor had only himself to blame.

Even so, Victor looked more vulnerable than I had seen him since his teeth extractions in college. As he sat in the shade of that oak tree, he looked like he needed to curl up on his mother's lap and have a good cry. He later told me that he knew he was going to jail.

* * *

My meeting was at one o'clock and his captain's meeting at two o'clock. Our plan was for him to keep the kids and meet me at the school to give them to me on the way to his captain's meeting. The time came, I asked one of the other PTF members to do the dismissal prayer and I left to met him on the sidewalk in front of the school. Still in a very pensive mood, he handed me the baby, and gave me a kiss along with a sheepish, "I'll see you later."

I remember that goodbye felt gentle. The sweetness of it took me by surprise. It reminded me of the old Victor. I stood there on that sidewalk, holding our baby and watched as his white Crown Victoria drove out of the parking lot and down the road. Soon he was out of sight. This was the last time that I would see him as a free man.

The next time I saw my husband, it was on television. He was being paraded on the television and led away in handcuffs escorted by two officers and placed in the back of a police car.

It was staggering.

The press had been informed to come to the mandatory captain's meeting because there was going to be a news story unlike any other in a long time. There was a prepared press release. It was orchestrated. Everybody was sure of what was to happen except the star of the show - Victor Thomas.

The captain's meeting had been a hoax, staged to get Captain Victor Thomas, the golden boy of the sheriff's department to report to the meeting for his arrest. They wanted no incidents, after all, Victor had threatened to kill people and they wanted the arrest to be secure. They also wanted to be sure the press was there to show what they do to their own when they betray the public trust.

Later, I asked one of the agents, "What would have happened if Victor had not responded to the call on the pager and not reported for the meeting?" Their response was that they would have tried to avoid coming to the house to arrest him if at all possible. But would have if necessary.

The golden boy was now tarnished and surely headed to prison for somewhere between 15 years to life.

All of these thoughts took me back to the conversation on the phone with my mother. I'll never in all my life forget that day. The crushing shock of it will never fade from the core of my memory.

"...No. He's not dead. But you need to come straight home. I can't tell you while you're driving. And take the kids over to D'Juna's house before you come home."

"Why? Why do I need to drop them off? Is Victor dead, Mama?" "No, he's not dead, come home and there will be people here to tell you what is going on."

The phone went dead.

I was not convinced.

On the way home, I planned his funeral. I planned what I was going to tell the kids. I questioned God about how I was going to raise five kids alone. I lived with the agonizing grief of losing my husband in death, and I pondered how I was going to tell my babies that their father was never coming home.

I lived with the death of my husband until I finally made it home.

When I arrived at my house there were two unmarked police cars in the driveway. One belonged to a longtime friend and former partner of Victor's from the drug unit, Mike. The other car held two female officers I had never seen before. As I got out of my van, they exited their cars and all three approached me. I didn't let them say anything. I turned to them and braced myself for the answer as I asked, "Is Victor dead?"

"No, his health is probably as good as when you last saw him," one of the female officers answered. "Oh, really," I responded with surprise, and a moment of relief.

The presence of these officers at my home, coupled with the behavior of my mother, let me know that something devastating had happened. If Victor wasn't dead, then what was it? I began to think, I know the kids are okay, and my parents are safe at my house - what could it be?

Flashes of the day raced through my mind - Victor's melancholy mood, Victor in the shade of the oak tree, and Victor's last goodbye. I don't know why or where it came from, but I blurted out, "Is Victor going to jail?"

"Yes," they said in unison. "He's on his way to jail."

. "Come on in," I said.

They came into the house, introduced themselves, and presented their nice, bright, shiny and very official badges. One of the officers reminded me that she had worked with

Victor in the drug unit and babysat our oldest daughter when she was a baby. "Oh yeah, I remember," I replied.

Next they showed me the press release that began, "Victor Thomas, an 18-year veteran of the Orange County Sheriff's department had been arrested in the biggest corruption case in twenty years."

The officers began to share a few of the details - not many, because the case was still open - but I had a sketchy idea of what had happened and sketchy was all I needed at the time. They told me Victor had been dealing in counterfeit merchandise and transporting drugs. He had been under surveillance for six months, and they observed him making several trips to South Florida to transport the goods. On the day before the arrest, he had transported forty pounds, equivalent to eighteen kilos of cocaine to Miami with anticipation of being paid $1,000 for each kilo - $18,000.

As I listened, I became numb. Their words were almost surreal. Thankfully, they didn't ask many questions, and I didn't have many either. They did ask whether I had seen Victor with large amounts of money, which I hadn't. They asked me to turn over anything that belonged to the sheriff's department. One of the officers went upstairs with me and we collected all of his starched and nicely pressed uniforms, his belts and boots. I was thinking, "Here, you can take this, and that . . . and be sure not to miss this one." Maybe if I got rid of any memories of the sheriff's department, this all would get easier, a little more believable. It was like a cleansing of my house and a part of the hurt and pain I felt. I wanted nothing to do with any of it.

Then the officer asked for his gun. I told her that I didn't know anything about a gun. Victor never brought his guns in the house because of the kids. That was true, he never did. At the time, it was the only redeeming quality about him that I could think of.

While the officers were there, Malone, the undersheriff

called. I had been frantically trying to call him so he could explain what was going on. He was our friend, I thought it would be comforting to hear his voice. Surely he would tell me something different, that maybe Victor was in a big undercover sting operation and part of the plan was that he had to endure public humiliation and a few days in jail to bring others to justice. Perhaps he was calling to apologize to me that the kids and I had to be caught up into this and to just hold on tight, because it all would be over soon.

Malone, my husband's confidant, didn't say any of this. All of it was real and it would get worse, much worse, before there was an inkling of it getting better.

When I spoke to Malone, I shouted at him in anger, "You knew all this was going on and you just let it happen? You should have stopped it. Why didn't you? How could you just sit back and let it happen?" As I heard later, during this tirade from me, he broke into tears. I couldn't detect that in his voice, all he said was that if he had interfered in any way at all, that he would have lost his job. To this I replied, "Well isn't a friend worth it?" We said our good-byes and rushed to end the conversation.

He was very matter of fact. If compassion was there, I couldn't detect it in his voice . . . no overwhelming concern for me and the kids. This was disappointing to me. I would have thought that if anyone had been on my doorstep to help me with the news, that it would have been Malone.

We had been through some of the best and worst of times with his family. I always felt that if any family would be with us when we needed it, that it would be him and his family. I imagine all this had been very hard for Malone to watch. Even so, I could understand their response to Victor, and I didn't blame them, but not to me and the kids.

What did we do wrong to have them and other so-called friends in the sheriff's department act as if they had never known us? People who kissed our babies, helped us move, and invited us to cook-outs. Why wouldn't they call or send a card? One of the officers was quoted as saying, "We feel as though we would have helped a dirty cop." We had known many of these people since Victor was in the police academy. They knew we weren't responsible for Victor's follies.

Anyway, the female officers had done what they came to do and were on their way out when they paused to ask, "Mrs. Thomas, do you have any other questions?"

Hesitantly, I inquired, "Was there another woman involved?" They seemed reluctant but relieved to answer, "Yes, there was another woman involved." I left it at that, because I had a sense that along with money and drugs, there were usually women. One vice usually leads to another.

God knows when enough is enough. And on this day, I had enough information. I was coping with not only the words, but also the emotions and the horror of it all.

I did want and need the answers to many questions, but God would provide it in bits and pieces as He strengthened me to handle it. Right here was where I had to learn to trust God even more than before. There was much more information that would be presented to me over the coming months. God knew that He would reveal all the answers I needed in time - His time.

Mike stayed for a while. I was thankful that he had come. The irony of it was, Victor had asked for him to come, to tell me what was going on before I saw it on the news. Actually he had first asked for another friend to come and tell me, but that friend was also being relieved of duty, so the job fell on Mike. In fact, it was at his house, with his wife, that I had left the kids. I felt sorry for him in a way. I knew it was horrible for him to have been delegated this job. He was a fellow officer. He did his best to help me, even though he was dealing with his own sadness and anger.

Mike was our friend, our families had vacationed

together. He thought enough of us and especially Victor to ask us to be his son's godparents. He was Victor's closest partner in the drug unit back in the "Duke Boys" days. And now he was here to mourn with me the loss of my husband, no, not to death, but to his own selfish centered nature and his dances with the devil.

My parents also mourned the loss of Victor, the young man that they had taken into their family and their hearts. My mother wept as she listened to the female officers talking with me. She wept for the betrayal, the hurt and the pain that her daughter and grandchildren were now catapulted into. I was afraid of the physical toll this would take on my mother and father.

In addition, Ken, who had worked with Victor at the boot camp, came over to offer his assistance and comfort. We all prayed a long, intent prayer. My best description of the emotion that hung over this day was extreme sadness. There were so many phone calls that I had to constantly clear the voice mail on the land line and the cell phone. Many were in tears and didn't know what to say. The multitude of messages were basically the same, "Are you okay?" and "I'm so sorry, I can't believe it, what can I do?"

There was only one call during that time that was any different. Victor's sister Gail called and the first words which came tartly out of her mouth were, "Natalie, what is going on with Victor?" My answer to her was, "I thought you might know." My response seemed to have hit a nerve with her and from there we began a shouting match and I told her that my immediate priority was the protection of my children.

She was irrate that law officers had come over to talk with me and no one had come over to warn her about the news before she saw it on television. I told her that Victor had arranged for someone to come over to talk to me and I didn't know why he didn't do the same for her. She was angry that her mother might have seen it on TV and that if she had, Gail said that it would, "kill her." Thank God, his mother didn't see it on TV. It would have been horrific for her. Even with our distant relationship, I would not have wanted her to find out this way.

I again assured her that this was something her brother had arranged and I didn't have anything to do with it, but I was surely grateful that he had thought enough of his family to do that.

The conversation escalated when I told her that I needed to go take care of my kids, her angered bellow was, "Well, if we see what's going on with Victor, the kids will be okay, you've got your priorities wrong, you've got your priorities wrong!" She obviously had only one concern and it wasn't Victor's children, or his wife. It was Victor and only Victor.

She took the time to inform me of a few of my other inadequacies and we ended the conversation when I got tired of listening to her degrading comments and angrily told her to "Go to Hell." She never missed an opportunity to inform me of how inferior I always was. This would be only the first in a series of unpleasant and bitter encounters with her.

To say that it felt like a dream or like watching a made-for-television movie would not only be terribly cliche, but altogether inaccurate. Everything felt real but unbelievable at the same time . . . brutally sharp . . . painfully real. It was like being awakened from a deep sleep by blinding sunlight in the eyes, or a splash of cold water on the face. I was cruelly forced into a world full of unanswered questions, and fear of what lay ahead.

I felt stripped naked in public. No one deserves this kind of humiliation. It felt like I had come out of a toilet stall with my skirt caught up at the waist and everyone I passed snickered behind my back. Why didn't someone care about my family, my children enough to tell me that this was happening? Not for my sake or Victor's, but for my children. Didn't someone care enough to try to spare them some of this? Couldn't they have warned me days before so I could prepare them and myself for one of the most tragic events of their lives? Why was there so much emphasis on watching this man dig his own grave, and so little on protecting five innocent children? What happened to the "it takes a village" philosophy? Why didn't the village protect my children? There were people on the periphery who knew what was going on. If it takes a village to raise a child, then what does it take to protect them?

* * *

Life goes on and as I began to get back to my daily routines and social organizations, I would always have one pervasive thought, especially when I was with a large group of women. I would look around the room and think, how many of these women has my husband "hit on?" How many of them know someone that he has been involved with? How many of them were thinking, "If she only knew." How many thought, "She should have known," or "Her husband is such a dog." There might have even been those who thought, "Well if she can't keep him at home, then she deserves it."

People are so funny, and they can be so matter of fact, when it doesn't personally affect them. I wonder if their attitudes would be so cavalier if the shoe was on their foot?

To heck with the skeptics. I had done nothing wrong. I had done nothing more than be ignorant of just how dark the soul of my husband was. I continued to hold my head up and not take on the shame of my husband's actions. I did this to set an example for my children but moreover to start to redeem some of my self worth.

* * *

Nonetheless, all the thoughts that I could quiet during the day would wake me up in the middle of the night. I sat straight up in bed at 3:00 in the morning, remembering, BENEFITS. Victor was carrying the benefits. What would happen to our healthcare? Another night I woke up in a panic, thinking THE CAR. Victor had always taken care of the car repairs.

But, as I put my kids to bed, and sat in the quiet of the house I wondered what would happen to my children. What would happen to Krystal and Loren when they fall in love for the first time? Would they be able to trust men? Would they always live in fear of being deserted? What about Erika? Her birthday forever scarred by this event. Would she always feel overlooked? Would she ever be able to express what she feels? Little Victor. My one and only son. What would he become, not having had that male role model to look up to? How could his father teach him to be a Godly man, an honorable man, and a trustworthy man when he didn't appear to know these things for himself? And Kelli, precious baby Kelli who would spend her early years never knowing what life was like with a father at home. How was this fair to any of them? Why were we paying such a high price for one man's soul?

I knew I could not answer these questions. During those long sleepless nights, I resolved in myself that I would do all I could to help them through this. I wanted them to be emotionally whole and healthy. They needed me. And God knows I needed them.

* * *

Achieving normalcy was no easy task. News trucks were parked outside the house for the first couple of days following the arrest. I did all I could to keep the kids from their questions and lights, keeping them in the house 24 hours a day. We ordered pizza to be delivered to the house, only to open the door to some news woman with a microphone instead of the delivery boy with a large pepperoni. When we did leave the house, we got into the van in the garage and whisked past the cameras as quickly as possible. We all were prisoners.

The media interviewed some of the neighbors who were not aware of the day's events yet. They even interviewed some of the kids that my children played with. These kids were completely baffled by the reporter's questions. Thankfully, all the neighbors were very kind to my children. As children do, the neighborhood kids got over it very quickly and were eager to have my kids back on the neighborhood ball teams.

At the same time, my daughters who were in the 6th, 4th, and 1st grades, wanted to go back to school the following week. I was reluctant at first. My 1st and 4th graders went to The First Academy (TFA), and the school guidance counselor and I had spoken over the weekend. We agreed that she would go into their classrooms and discuss the events with the children, to properly prepare them for seeing Loren and Erika. I went into Loren's class with her and spoke to the children briefly about what was on the news and asked them if they had any questions. My thought was to run interference and have them ask me the questions instead of putting Loren in the position of having to struggle to give answers to something that she was still deciphering herself. The kids were ever so kind and forgiving, if only adults had the same spirit of forgiveness. There was never another word about it at TFA. They accepted us as if nothing had happened and put their efforts into helping us, not blaming us. It was all handled in such a Godlike manner. I will be forever grateful that they did not impose the sins of the father upon the children.

It wasn't so easy for my eldest. She was attending a

different school for the first time in her school years. We were new to this setting, unlike TFA. The administration and some of the parents, especially a friend of mine who had attended TFA with us, tried their best to do damage control and help Krystal get back in the swing of things.

There was one family who wanted their daughter to abruptly end the friendship with Krystal, fearing their daughter would be tainted by exposure to my daughter. I talked to the mother and told her among other things that, "I hoped her perfect little world would always stay neat and tidy." She called her husband, crying and upset about our conversation. I informed him too, that I often heard him talk of God and he purported to be a Christian, so how could he lead his family in these actions against my daughter? I wasn't going to change his mind, and he wasn't going to change mine. We ended the conversation on an amicable note. It was disconcerting for Krystal and it just broke my heart.

I began to feel sorry for the girl because she seemed to have genuinely liked my daughter. She seemed confused with how she wanted to act, and how she was told to act by her parents. I knew that somewhere in the life of this girl, she would face another situation, maybe not exactly like this one, but in time God would reveal to her the shallowness of her parents' thinking.

What a cruel lesson to have to learn at such a young age. What a heavy dose of reality to have to swallow. I suppose there are some people who actually do believe in guilt by association and I had just met two of them. I just wanted to keep Krystal home with me. I considered this. But, in my heart, I knew however hard that I couldn't always protect my children from the challenges that real life often brings. Her best protection would be from God. I would help Krystal through this time and she would be stronger in the end for it. Krystal also had many classmates who advocated her case against the "untouchable girl." Krystal had support from her classmates, her peers, whom she needed the most to understand her.

When the kids were at school and the younger two were occupied, I'd allow my mind to wander. At times I'd think about all that had been taken away from us, and I could feel beginnings of self-pity. I wanted the husband, the family, the household as it was, the family outings . . . I wanted my dream back. But I felt that barring a miracle, it would not happen. There were even times at night that I would still hear Victor coming up the steps. Then I would realize it was just a dream that would never come true again.

Then I would think about Victor. Through my anger, I really pitied him. I could only imagine the level of inner torment he was experiencing as the two sides of him dueled it out for dominance. When two sides battle, there is always a winner. You always hope the winner is the good side. It made me sad to think of his turmoil, the conflict that must have driven him over the edge, away from all that had been right in his life. At the same time I was angry because he had taken his family over the edge with him. He had no right to do this.

I could picture the little cartoon angel and devil on the bulldog's shoulder . . . "Go ahead, smash the frying pan over the cat's head," "No, make friends with the cat, shake his hand," "Smash him," "Love him" . . . The frying pan usually won.

Despite all my disappointment, I still held onto an ounce of hope that we could be restored as a family, but only if it was God's will. I held onto a slight chance that this man would look up, look around, and accept responsibility for what he had done. I held on to hope in God who is so much bigger than any force of evil that might be controlling Victor. I held on to hope that in this story, in our story, the sacredness of family would triumph for God's glory.

Yet that hope was elusive . . . so hard to hold on to.

When something was going wrong, my mother used to always tell me to, "Get a good night's sleep and it would be better in the morning." This wasn't getting any better, over the days and weeks following his arrest, little by little the story unfolded before me.

How many women have felt betrayal in their marriages? How many women will take and take and take to try to keep their families together? We know there is another side, and we persevere without being sure what waits for us. We endure pain, and sacrifice just trying to get to the other side. How many of us are willing to give up who we are? How many of us leave it all on the line for our families? How many of us hate the feeling of sleeping alone? Of making decisions without a partner? Of only one toothbrush in the toothbrush holder?

Unfortunately, for some men, the oldest trick in the book is make the wife look mentally unbalanced. I knew of many female friends who were accused of being "crazy" by their wayward spouses. It was this way with Victor Thomas. I read the incriminating words in letters he had written to his sister and my mother. I'm sure these weren't the only letters, but they were enough to uncover his plot.

The first time I learned of his intent to make me look unbalanced, it was crushing. The next time it was comical. I just thought, "He never stops trying to manipulate." I let it go.

What more could he do to me? By this time, he had done it all. There was nothing left, but to discredit me to the ones who would listen.

I did resent him using my mother, although I saw right through the method to his madness. He knew that the relationship between me and my mother struggled, and probably felt she was easy prey. If she listened to him long enough to discredit me, then it would leave room for him to come in and save the day. For two elderly people, who were in the twilight of their lives, they might even feel gracious enough to share part of the assets that they had worked so hard for.

Fear, and greed are two powerful motivators.

Indeed sometimes, when we have been emotionally and or physically abused for years, we might appear temporarily unstable. When your self worth is constantly battered, and you are emotionally bruised, then you do become unbalanced. You have to fight to find your center again as you struggle to regain that balance and trust in yourself.

It isn't easy.

Many of us in this situation constantly second-guess ourselves, having long ago lost the security to believe in our own decisions. Our self-confidence has been systematically chipped away, until there is little left. We begin to think that everyone is better than we are and make better decisions. It begins to be an uphill battle to be self-reliant again.

What's so ironic is that given the right situation, isolation from loved ones, and a manipulative twist of words by an endearing con-man, and sometimes we do look a bit mentally deficient. It's all a game. If we look deranged then it's a better excuse for our spouse's ill intended actions. The worse we look in the eyes of others, the better they look. There will always be a few that they could a make a case to. There are probably some incidents that have made us look insane but in the end, the truth will always reveal itself.

To try to paint a picture of us as being less than the strong women and mothers that we are meant to be is a cheap shot.

As Christian women, we have an even deeper perspective. A more grounded perspective. Sometimes we are willing to stay in our marriages because we see it as a covenant made before God. We know that our judgement is not by earthly measures, so we keep moving forward and pray.

For some people, I might seem foolish, but I knew that if I was to be released from this marriage, it would only be in

God's time, not mine. I would be released when God helped me understand the lessons He was trying to teach me.

Without a doubt, for me, the words for the news of the arrest were horror and disbelief. I felt sucked into a vacuum with no one to shut off the power. I felt pulled by forces beyond my control into a deep dark underground that had never seen the light of day. I was in shock. How do you react to having your life take a U-turn in an instant? What are the emotions for this? How do you solve this? How do you sort through it? Who helps you do this? Whom do you talk to?

There was no more denying, no more hiding the facts under the rug, it was everywhere, on television, in the newspapers, being talked about in restaurants, and in the hair salons.

Hair salons have always been a place of gossip. Now, my family was the subject. I wasn't too concerned about this, because I had long since resolved that I was not going to allow my house to be covered in shame. I wasn't going to teach my children to accept that. I knew that in a short time, my news would be old news and the gossip mill would find another subject. My kids and I had a bigger and badder ally on our side - God. And He could fight any of our battles.

* * *

When Victor was first arrested, I held onto the wish that he would be released on bail very soon. I didn't know how much it would cost, or where we would get the money, but I wanted him home. I wanted him home to look me in the face to answer questions. It wasn't going to happen. Anytime the subject of bail came up, the prosecuting attorney said that she would bring out the "dirty stuff." By that she meant she would reveal things that might further hurt the family. It never happened. The defense attorney also told me that the evidence against Victor was "too damning."

Soon my wish for bail was a long, lost dream too.

They also refused to set bail because they feared he was a flight risk. He had spoken of acquaintances that he had in other parts of the country, so they felt like he needed to stay right where he was.

I wanted to believe that all the events would bring about a change in Victor and for a while, I was sure that it would. Surely, his face on the evening news, being led away in handcuffs in front of his co-workers, having the press right there to catch every expression and all this being played every half hour on the television would humble any man. Knowing that he would miss many of the formative years of his children's lives by being stuck away in a prison would be sobering. Surely his only thought would be to make all this up to his family. This had to be temporary insanity, or an exaggerated mid-life crisis. Maybe he even had a mental break from reality.

Yet, still it was important to me that I stand by him. Within myself, I had to know that I hadn't abandoned him at this time. To me, this was the through thick and thin, for better or worse part of our marriage vows. Did this man deserve my loyalty or commitment?

I had so many mixed thoughts during this time. "How could he do that to us? . . . How would this all end?" . . . "Where did the lies begin and end?" . . . "Why didn't I see it coming?" . . . "Why wasn't I good enough?" . . . "How much blame was I allowing myself to accept?" But, the most comforting thought I had was, "I know God is going to stand by me."

Another theory that I never accepted was that he was performing the criminal acts to benefit his family in some way. We were living in the aftermath of his destruction and this was a long way from feeling beneficial. It felt more like sacrificial. According to the investigators, most of the money was spent outside the family, either taking girlfriends on lavish weekend trips, or spending it at the bars while socializing.

Still, my most overwhelming thought was, "How could he do this to us?" I couldn't get this off my mind. Sometimes this question would take over my thoughts, and go around and around in my head . . . why? . . . Why? . . . WHY?

I began to feel that only a man who was out of his mind would allow his life and the lives of six others who deserved his protection, to get so out of control. I also knew that if he didn't know the answers before now, then it was a must for him to get some serious psychological counseling.

My husband had become everything I thought he'd **never** be.

PHOTOS

Wedding photo of Victor and Natalie

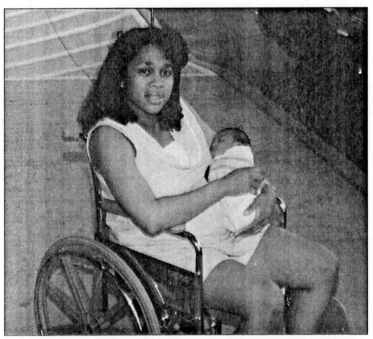

Natalie leaving the hospital with newborn baby Loren

Victor and little Vic skiing on the bunny slope

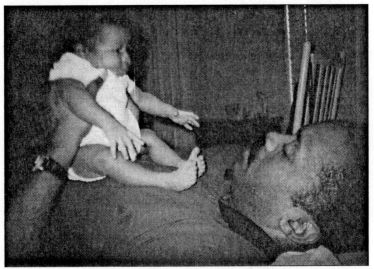

Victor holding newborn baby Kelli

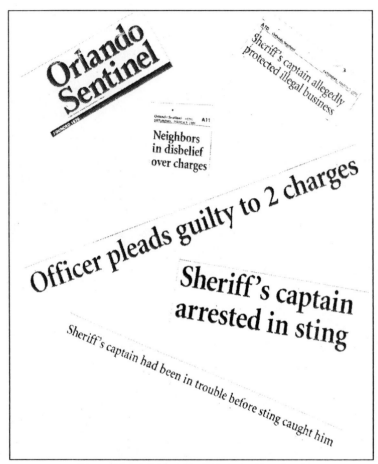

Headlines from the Orlando Sentinel

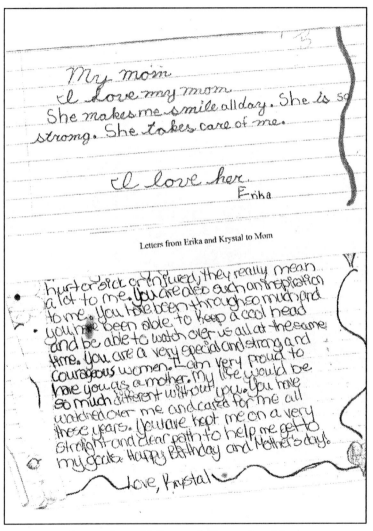

My mom

I love my mom.
She makes me smile all day. She is so
strong. She takes care of me.

I love her.

Erika

Letters from Erika and Krystal to Mom

...hurt or sick or confused, they really mean
a lot to me. You are also such an inspiration
to me. You have been through so much and
you've been able to keep a cool head
and be able to watch over us all at the same
time. You are a very special and strong and
courageous women. I am very proud to
have you as a mother. My life would be
so much different without you. You have
watched over me and cared for me all
these years. You have kept me on a very
straight and clear path to help me get to
my goals. Happy Birthday and Mother's day!

Love, Krystal

Letter from Erika and Krystal to Mom

Natalie white water rafting in Tennessee

Natalie and Kelli sharing a kiss on Natalie's 46th birthday

CHAPTER 7

A New Reality

"There are six things the Lord hates - no, seven things he
detests: haughty eyes, a lying tongue, hands that kill the
innocent, a heart that plots evil, feet that race to do wrong,
a false witness who pours out lies, a person who sows
discord among brothers."

Proverbs 6:16-19

Even though I had been alone before - even though
Victor had been absent in both mind and body throughout the last few years of our marriage, it was different this
time. Everything was different. The regular routines
remained — school, sports practice, diaper changing, homework. But now I had a new reality. My husband was a felon.

People are accustomed to divorce and even death, but
incarceration holds a different stigma. Having an incarcer-
ated father and husband is not "socially acceptable." Though
people were kind, I was continually reminded of this label,
especially when we visited him in the Seminole County jail.

Visiting a jail was a different world. There were only

certain days that we could visit and only certain times - Saturday nights and Thursday mornings. The length of the visit was at the discretion of the guards. We were in their world and we had to follow their rules. Seminole County jail was a holding facility for federal prisoners, where they were housed until sentencing. He was in isolation for the whole seven months - only Victor and God (or the devil) in his cell.

Yet, still I was in too much pain to feel sorry for him. I fluctuated between hurt, anger, pity, and hatred. I knew the only emotion that God wanted me to express was forgiveness, but I was struggling with that and God knew it. I was torn with knowing how God wanted me to act and actually doing it. During some visits I was so full of fury that I would draw Victor to tears. I couldn't hold back. Then I would pray and by the next visit, I would have enough peace to have a pleasant conversation. But that was short lived. I was reminded of our reality when I reached out to touch the thick glass that separated us with one hand and held onto the phone to talk to him with the other.

At one point during all these visits, I saw some of the old Victor start to resurface, the Victor I knew years before. He seemed remorseful, sensitive, open. This didn't last long. Looking back, I think these were emotions of fear. Victor had often expressed fear over the number of years he would be sentenced, and where he might end up. Toward the end of the seven months, he reverted to the Victor that got him into this predicament.

He seemed less willing to explore the depths of his emotions and accept responsibility for all of his actions. The key word is "all." He was willing to accept partial responsibility and was looking to share the remainder with someone else, anyone else in his path, mainly me. I saw the walls of deception and lies come up again as his attorney was preparing for his defense. The "what can you do for me" attitude began to reemerge.

All in all, some of the guards were very nice and some were very stern. I got to know their personalities, the more I visited. You'd know if you were going to get an hour visit or a half hour visit just by seeing who was on duty. They all seemed quite understanding of the kids and one female guard was very friendly to my little son. She used to say, "It's bad enough that they are separated from their father and have to visit him in here, so I'll try to let you visit as long as possible." The kids and I were very thankful for her compassion. The kindness of some of the guards made the whole visitation easier to bear.

Although the kids were always excited about the two visits a week to see their father, and looked forward to it, they did not look forward to talking to him through the glass. It was strange for them. Kids need touch — hugs and kisses. The jail administrator was a very empathetic man and allowed us three "contact visits." This was a huge favor made out of the kindness of his heart. He allowed us one for Mother's Day, Victor's birthday and one right before he left this facility to be transported to his final sentencing facility.

Yes, I wondered what was going through the minds of my children — having to talk to their Dad through glass and see him in the orange jumpsuit that prisoners wear.

At times, I was so angry that I felt like screaming at him for having us in this circumstance.

Visiting an inmate is a world that I had never been exposed to before and had never imagined being part of. There were many different kinds of people waiting to spend some time with their loved ones. Some, like us, were obviously trying to find their way in this new alien world. Others were apparently pretty used to the system and it was just another visit for them.

It is unfortunate that sin is so prevalent and consumes so many families. There were old people, babies, toddlers, teens, unborn babies, mothers, fathers, sisters and brothers there, all caught up in a system that at times seems almost inhumane. It was right here during this time that I knew there were no real lines of society.

There was no one better than another. We are all subject to sin and destruction. No amount of education, exposure, or material things can protect you against the snares of the world, only God can do that. After all, we were good people who lived right, didn't bother anyone and went to church. How did we ever get here?

* * *

After the arrest, I needed answers. I needed to try to figure out what happened. I decided to go down and read the surveillance transcripts kept by the F.B.I. and sheriff's department. I began to find the information that brought me to reality. Up until reading the shockingly real words, I refused to fully admit what others were telling me. I could do that no longer. It was ironic that in the surveillance transcripts, the code name for Victor was " Magic."

In the surveillance transcripts I read about the man with a dual personality. A man with two lives. I often recall the prosecutor's comments on the day of sentencing, "There are two Victor Thomases."

One day when I went to the F.B.I. office to read transcripts, I asked one of the agents, "What do you think is important to Victor," and his candid, spontaneous reply was, "Victor." I chuckled, and asked again, "Well, after Victor, what do you think is important to him?" Again, his quick response was, "Victor." I laughed out loud, because the agent was so serious, and so intent on, "Nothing is more important to Victor than Victor."

The task force agents observed as Victor slipped further and further under the surface of the water, into the depths of criminal activity and adultery. Two of the officers expressed to me that they were "disgusted" by what they saw. They described to me a time when there was an "officer down" call that went across the police radio. All officers respond to this. The surveillance team observed Captain Victor Thomas who should have been one of the first on the scene, in a restaurant sitting having dinner, watching TV, and ignoring the call. They felt he had no respect for his family, or his fellow officers and behaved as though "Victor was the center of the universe."

This was when I first learned of the woman that Victor had lived with. His former girlfriend who had filed the charges against him back in 1999, seemed to relish in a tone of revenge as she ranted in front of the television cameras on the day of the arrest saying, "Who do you believe now, who do you believe now?"

I was also convinced that Victor had some money hidden away. I believed this money to be managed by his sister. I wasn't the only one who believed this. I also chose not to become preoccupied about Victor's hidden stash. If he had money hidden for himself, and knew that his family could use the financial assistance, then that was another matter between Victor and God. God provided for our needs, no matter what Victor had set aside.

I began to learn so many things that had been covered under lies, secrets and deception for so many years. Though I am convinced that even the transcripts will never reveal everything that my husband was capable of.

From the surveillance material, I read that Victor Thomas was found by the F.B.I, to have a non-conventional religious practice, wherein he put the names of his enemies on a sheet of paper in coffee grounds. This list was found in his police car upon his arrest. The names of Orange County personnel and ex-girlfriends were on this list. I asked them if I was on this list, and they told me, No. Anyone who professes to know God has absolutely no business delving into the pit of witchcraft. After having a conversation with one of Victor's ex-roommates from college who is now a well-respected minister, I was reminded that even back during our college days, Victor had an interest in "power," wherever it might come from.

I had not known my husband at all. Who was this man who used to wear a T-shirt saying "Real Men Pray Everyday," and got on his knees before going to bed? Whom was he praying to? What was he praying for? He was an enigma.

Further, as I learned more about him and got answers to questions I had never wanted to ask, the thought of ever being reconciled with him was buried deeper and deeper by thin sheets of white paper covered with lines of painfully revealing words. The more pages of the transcripts I read, the more painful the news.

Reading the transcripts answered a lot of questions. Although I knew that I would never have the answers to all my questions or know all of my husband's unGodly deeds.

I could now go back and put that puzzle together and make the pieces fit. It was with great sadness that I read through page after page of unbelief. But also, there was a sense of relief. It helped me to let go. It began to help free me from the bondage of trying to hold on to something that had been out of my control for a long time.

The transcripts initiated another important process for me. It helped me release myself from blame. I began the process of believing in myself again, because I knew beyond a shadow of a doubt, that I had no responsibility for the actions of Victor Thomas.

This was like a burden lifted for me. I could now forgive myself. I could face the truth and find the strength to move on. I was beginning to see what God was teaching me all along — that He would help me fight my battles in time, His time.

CHAPTER 8

Destruction of a God-given Gift

". . . whatever is true, whatever is noble, whatever is right, whatever is pure, whatever is lovely, whatever is admirable - if anything is excellent or praiseworthy - think on these things."

Phillippians 4:8

God what am I going to do?
All of the ups and downs during this time kept my spirit unsettled. At times I was paralyzed with fear, wondering how I was going to make it through. I didn't sleep all night for weeks and months at a time and grew more and more emotionally and physically exhausted. At times I was so angry I could hardly contain it. But during these low times I was continually buoyed by an ever strengthening relationship with God.

I had experienced a death in my home, my marriage and I needed to mourn it.

Not only did I have to contend with visiting my husband

in jail, but in April of the same year, a month after Victor was arrested, my father was told that he needed to have a quadruple heart bypass. The same day that I was at the doctor's office getting the news about my father, Betty, Victor's oldest sister called to tell me that their mother died. I felt bad for all of us. I knew that God was seriously trying to get our attention, and He was determined to get it.

Yes, I ached for my father. He had always been so strong. So invincible. Now as they wheeled him into the operating room, he seemed so vulnerable. He smiled at my mother and me as he was wheeled down that hallway. He entered the operating room, so proudly, so fearlessly, and never came out the same. The father that I had all my life, had a tough recovery from his surgery. Subsequently, he had a minor stroke. The man that always had an ear for me, always made me feel special, and always loved me so unconditionally was not the same. I missed him, and who he used to be.

I was reminded again of the relationship I had found with God in the lonely times of 1997. He became more than a mythical story or just someone I prayed to before a meal. My faith moved beyond a religion into the personal relationship that it was always supposed to be. I heard once in a sermon that "the shortest distance between your problems and the solution is the distance between your knees and the floor." It was so true.

I remember the friend who had been a spiritual mentor to me, told me in 1997 that, "No real tragedies have ever come to your life." He said that I was just cutting my spiritual teeth through the experience of our troubled marriage and that God was preparing me for something bigger. He was getting me ready. I disregarded this notion, for I thought that with what I was going through then, being separated from my husband, living in a small apartment with four young kids, and feeling bad about myself was pretty awful. I couldn't imagine much worse. But this friend was so right on.

I was eternally grateful for the foundation of faith I had formed during my earlier spiritual battles. As one minister used to say, "You have to stay prayed up for the storms of your life." It was my relationship with God, without a doubt, that brought me through the wild waves of changing emotions. It was the prayers, reading the Bible story of Job who lost everything but his physical life. The stories of Ruth, David, Paul, the support of fellow believers and the love of my children. All of this strengthened my resolved to move on.

One of my favorite stories was in Mark 4:35, when Jesus calmed the storm. The disciples thought Jesus was not aware of the storm - that He didn't care, as He was sleeping in the boat. They asked Him, "Teacher, don't you care if we drown?" Jesus then asked them "Why are you so afraid? Do you still have no faith?"

Jesus is with us through the storms of our lives. Many times it seems as though He is quiet and not paying attention, but many times it is in His silence that He is doing the greatest work. Through this story, He taught His disciples faith, in the midst of a storm.

I could not quit and give up the fight. I had to ride out this storm and rely on Jesus for guidance and strength. We all need Jesus in our boat through the storms of life.

* * *

One emotion remained unchanged. It gave me the greatest torment and it came from the depth of my soul, from a deep dark place that is too painful to touch. Its name is remorse. I had a gut-wrenching remorse for what Victor had done, to me, to his children, and to the African-American community as a whole.

For that reason, I felt his self-absorption put us back to a place many had fought to escape from for generations. Ken also felt that "Victor set Black men back thirty years." Black men like Victor help to confirm a stereotype, that all Black men are inherently criminals and liars. There are many men who disprove this stereotype, including my own father. He was a role model for me and I thought that what I saw in him, could be expected of the man I married. There are many Black fathers and professional men who I look up to and prove every day that our validation does not lie in the hands of others. These are men who have worked hard for what they have, and are a great example for the community, their families, and their co-workers. They are honorable, trustworthy, and hardworking.

For all those who thought Victor was different because he was well-educated, well-spoken, ambitious and charming, he proved for some that this was not enough. Victor had it all on the outside, but evidently not enough on the inside, to stop him from resorting to the same criminal behavior that he arrested people for.

During slavery, marriages were not recognized by law, though they were encouraged because a married slave was less likely to run away. If a deal was made to sell a slave, the slave was sold, without regard for family ties. Husbands were torn from wives, wives from husbands, and children from their mothers. Many slaves risked their lives to return to their families. Some never saw the children born to them, and many children never knew their fathers. Such atrocities and inhumane treatment are what men fought and died for in wars and on the streets.

Victor had a gift, a God-given gift which he tore apart by his own actions, bad choices and self serving ambitions. He didn't have any more value for a family than the slave masters. He was willing to throw away his family when we held no more worth. When our purpose was served, our value was gone. He wanted to trade us in for better. He made a mockery of those who sacrificed for us to live better and for men like Victor Thomas to taste success.

Similarly, my parents worked hard to provide an opportunity for me. They saved and budgeted so I could go to college and get a good job to be independent. Their wish was for me to take care of myself and to be a good and productive citizen. They also wished for me to marry a man who would respect, protect, and provide for me and do the same for our children. They felt that they had raised a daughter worthy of this.

But now, how am I different? According to the 2000, 47.1% of black households are headed by single women, as opposed to 14.5% of white households. A 1999 Forum on Child and Family Statistics stated that 64% of all black children live in single parent homes. My children and I are now part of these statistics, despite all we had going for us to break the pattern. According to the Bureau of Prisons, 40.5% of federal prisoners are black men — 54.7% of them imprisoned for drug offenses. Victor too has become a statistic.

Ironically, the sheriff's department looked up to him. Many of the young black men coming up in the ranks saw him as their idol, the one whom they aimed to model their careers after. What do they think now? Has Victor crushed all of their hope for future success?

I particularly grieve the influence Victor's actions had on the young men he worked with at the boot camp. He was a mentor to many of those boys, once again, standing out as an example of what they could become if they worked hard and got their act together.

Victor was a small town boy who rose through the ranks. He himself was an against the odds story. But with all the help and breaks that he was given, he was not stronger or better than anyone else at escaping the pitfalls of life. His education was no insulation for the demons inside waging war to indulge in women, drugs, and other criminal activity. He couldn't escape the lures and lies of greed and power. The lies of Satan.

I remember the story of one boy whose mother was dying of AIDS while he was in the boot camp. Victor pulled all kinds of strings to personally take this boy to the nursing home to say goodbye to his mother. At the boot camp graduation, Victor singled the boy out, and gave him a special award as one that was able to overcome obstacles and survive. What did that boy think when he saw Victor's face on the news? What happened to the validity of Victor's words of encouragement? What about Victor's words to stay away from crime? Did the boy ever read the ironic statement in the paper, that Victor's own mother died while he was in prison?

Sadly, Victor is guilty of what so many men and women in America are guilty of. They have no concept of the far-reaching effects of their actions. They have no insight, or "outsight" of the world around them, living in a self-centered existence, falsely believing that what they do is their own business. They believe they are invincible, untouchable, entitled to do what they want and seem incapable of sincere empathy. The technical word for this impairment is narcissism. It's really the modern tragedy of our time. These people feel they are entitled to engage in every sinful act they desire.

I am not claiming to have proven scientific facts of the mental state of my husband, but I am expressing my views as an observer of a condition that adversely affected my life. When I contemplated the extent of Victor's disregard for the people in his life, and lack of empathy after his arrest, I began to feel that there was something more.

Who was this man that transported eighteen kilos of cocaine to Miami and then walked in to celebrate his daughter's birthday as if nothing had happened? Are these the actions of a sane person? How could he come in and celebrate with us, take pictures with us, share birthday cake and bring in gifts as if it had been an ordinary day at the office? There had to be another explanation.

I wondered if there was some sort of mental impairment that made him unable to really "feel" what he had done, to take total responsibility. He couldn't seem to connect the dots between his actions and the consequences. It was almost like, "He didn't get it."

I began to read books and articles about the personality disorder of narcissism and its characteristics. I saw many similarities between the cases described and Victor himself. The primary characteristic of narcissism is self centeredness. According to the <u>DSM-IV</u> (Diagnostic and Statistical Manual of Mental Disorders, fourth editions), there are nine characteristics of a narcissist. According to the text from <u>Malignant Self Love - Narcissism Revisited</u>, someone with NPD (Narcissistic Personality Disorder), "Requires excessive admiration, adulation, attention and affirmation or, failing that, wishes to be feared and to be notorious (narcissistic supply)." I remembered the threat to the informant's family. Another characteristic that seemed especially applicable was, ". . . <u>uses</u> others to achieve his or her own ends." This seemed to be a pervasive trait in my husband. Another pattern that the narcissist repeats is to idealize, devalue and discard, especially with the significant other. This too seemed to fit Victor Thomas. The serial affairs, the excessive need for control, resistance to accept total responsibility and the expectations of entitlement, all were characteristics that I saw in Victor. I was convinced he had NPD, more specifically, somatic narcissism (derive their narcissistic supply from their physique, exercise, physical or sexual prowess and "conquests").

The prognosis for an adult narcissist is poor, though his adaptation to life and to others can improve with treatment. Also, the narcissist almost always uses the significant other as the unfortunate scapegoat.

We have begun to accept narcissistic behavior as normal and acceptable - redefining it as self-fulfillment and the old "I just want to be happy" syndrome.

How is it justified that one person's happiness is justification for destroying a family? Seek God and His will and look into the faces of the children and honestly ask yourself if you are destroying their family so that they will be happy or for you to fulfill your earthly desires. I believe this has to change if we want to survive as a society.

In a January 1998 news article, Victor was quoted as saying, "The problem we have with juveniles is they don't think there are any consequences." He went on to say, "They commit a crime, and they get slapped on the wrist. They have to commit five or six crimes before they get bumped up in the system." This time it wasn't a juvenile offender that these words applied to, now it was Captain Victor Thomas, an 18-year seasoned professional, father and husband.

By now I understood what to expect when one of Victor's sisters said to me, "Well, when Victor gets out there can be another marriage and there can be more children." I asked her if she was advocating that Victor just discard his wife and kids, and she replied, "It may sound cruel, but if his wife and kids keep causing him pain, then he might just need to move on. And he can have another wife and he'll still be young enough to have more kids." Why would my family be important if the people who surround Victor think that families are disposable? When it gets too tough and painful, then you just throw them away and "make another."

One of Victor's current adulteresses had a lot to tell me during a phone call. He told me about her after he was arrested. I say one of his adulteresses because it is clear from the transcripts, as the investigators put it, "He cheated on her just as badly as he cheated on me." She told me that the only reason she was talking to me was because she was a

Christian, because her best friend told her to curse me out and hang up. How noble of her. She started with, "I'm a Christian but . . ." There is no double-jointed set of standards for being a Christian. There should be no "buts."

She told me that she was in love with my husband and he was in love with her and they were going to be together when he got out. She told me that I was his wife in name only. She also told me that they just used me during the court hearing to reduce Victor's sentence and the week he was arrested, he was going to ask me for a divorce.

On that comment, I laughed inside but didn't want to say anything that would stop her roll and I wanted to hear what else she had to say. But, I was thinking, "Well doesn't that tell you something? If Victor was going to ask me for a divorce this week, which I doubt, but just in case he was, God sent you two a mountain sized message." There was still some humor to be found in this menagerie of dirt.

She told me that he had so many things at her house that it looked like he was moving in. She said that he wrote and called her constantly and told her that he would go crazy if it wasn't for her. She wanted me to believe that she tried to end the relationship, but "Victor ain't hearing that, Victor ain't hearing that." She spoke of their sex life and that the only reason she wasn't pregnant was because she insisted on the birth control. That Victor didn't care if she got pregnant and he'd often say, "Baby we'll just make our own." She said that she never felt like the other woman because he treated her like a "queen." There was glibness in her tone when she let me know that Victor never called my name and only referred to me as the "Mother of his children."

Yes, all this was hard to hear, but I had to. It was sinful and disgusting, but I had to know. I knew she would tell her version of the truth whereas a man practicing this type of deception would only continue to lie, if it benefitted him. When I mentioned some of the things she said to me, Victor denied much of it and said that she was just being the other woman and taking her opportunity to take jabs at me. He used to always say that if she would only tell me the truth that she would tell me that nothing came before his family.

More of the truth is, everything came before his family.

He said that I should be careful of what she would say to me. He also firmly stated many times that he had no intentions of ever doing anything upon his release except coming home. He used to say I gave her too much credit. By now, it didn't matter to me if all of it was true or not. One line of truth was too much.

Coupled with all the information that she so graciously gave me, I found out that his sister again was involved. I found the woman's phone number at Gail's house. When I called her, she informed me that, "I know how to get in touch with Gail anytime I want."

When I confronted Gail, she lied and claimed she didn't know who this person was and that her son had written the number after taking a message. She was cooking, and I saw her hands shaking as she struggled with what to say to cover the trail. I could only venture to guess, what would happen next?

It didn't feel good, but we were still trying to make a semblance of family. I took three of my five children up to Yazoo prison to visit their father one weekend and who comes into the visiting room - his adulteress accompanied by his sister. I was shocked that either of the three of them would do this to the children, me and themselves.

I didn't react very much because by now I had almost become immune to shock. I began to just wait on what was lurking around the corner just waiting to jump out next.

I did not argue, and I did not act upset because I didn't want my children to figure out who this woman was. I told them that it was a friend of Gail's and at the time they seemed to believe that.

I was later told that Gail wanted this to happen. Victor's oldest sister Betty wanted to stop the encounter because she thought it was wrong. I thank Betty for that.

Never mind that Gail knew my children would be there. Forget taking into consideration the unknown of how any of us would react in this collision. What mattered to Gail was that her brother be allowed the chance to make a decision - not to do the right thing, but for him to have a choice. There were other ways to accomplish the same purpose if Gail wanted fireworks, but it didn't have to be in front of my children. The setting was prison, young children are around, and their father nor their aunt had enough decency to avoid exposing them to such a painful situation. There was a part of me right then and there that decided these people were not worth it. There really was some sickness here that I did not need to be a part of.

Looking back, my two older daughters did not want to go to Yazoo that weekend. They said they just had a funny feeling and didn't want to go, so they didn't, and I didn't force them. Thank God, they didn't need this in their faces. Their instincts were much better than mine. Out of the mouths of babes.

Figuratively, if I had a gun, I would have shot him.

Inside, I was angry and disgusted. All I wanted to do was be angry. I was so angry that I couldn't feel my spiritual growth. I was consumed with anger. I had to rise above it and not give in to this consuming emotion. It was not productive for me and it wouldn't change anything.

Temporarily, I stopped praying, and I stopped talking to God. I talked more to my anger, but I knew this had to change. The Bible says to not let the sun go down on your anger, and I let many suns go down on the anger in my heart. It didn't feel good, and it didn't feel right. I knew I had to be the one to change. There had to be one less player in this masquerade, and for the sake of me and my children, it had to be me, and it had to be now.

I could not spend another thought, another letter, another visit on this man. All I could do now was to pray that he found God and when he did, that he didn't try to manipulate God too. If there was any time in my life that I thought I was better than anyone, it was now — I was undoubtedly better than this and I needed to start acting like it. It was long, long past time.

I prayed to God for strength and guidance and to help me understand and rise above all this. I prayed for God to remove the anger from my heart. It became a daily prayer. I asked many others to pray this for me also. I meditated on my favorite scripture, ". . . whatever is true, whatever is noble, whatever is right, whatever is pure, whatever is lovely, whatever is admirable - if anything is excellent or praiseworthy - think about such things." (Phillipians 4:7) There was nothing here that was any of these things.

I also added one more prayer—to remove Victor from my heart. I wanted the feelings gone and I wanted God to release me from my commitment to the marriage. I had never prayed this before, but I was praying it now. That was the final straw on the camel's back - I didn't want it anymore. And I wanted nothing to do with Victor. Furthermore, she could have him. They deserved each other. But I knew that no matter how I felt, I needed God to be the one who said that it was okay. It had to be in God's timing, no matter how hurt or angry I was.

Since this incident in July of 2002, I have decided that it is better for me if I do not communicate with Victor. I do not go to visit him. He has contact with his children via the phone and letters. His absolute disregard for anyone's needs but his own led me to the conclusion that I needed to let him go, completely, in order to allow God to do with me and with him what He wills. I could not continue to be hurt and dragged down in this quagmire of his foolishness. I had to make a choice to move on or move down. I chose on. I chose up.

It was liberating . . .

Adultery is wrong. No ifs, ands, or buts about it, as my mother would say. It sends a myriad of unGodly messages. It is one sin that God hates the most, because it is the one sin that you commit against your own body, and the one sin that devastates all involved. You don't commit adultery in isolation. It will all come out one day, and when it does, it is nothing short of destructive.

How can any marriage be Godly when so many strangers are in bed with you? You can't bring the essence of so many persons into your home and expect it to survive. Victor had an obligation to keep our household untainted and safe.

Looking back, why did Victor feel driven to commit so much infidelity? Only Victor himself can explain this. I can speculate on a few ideas. Was it the thrill of some new encounters, some new conquests, was it the thrill of the chase? Was it the narcissism? Had life at home gotten so overwhelming, so uneventful, so mundane? Could I not compare to the "girls" who had time to sit in a nail salon for hours and match their nail polish to their newly purchased outfits? Had we grown so far in different directions that we no longer cared to hear each other? Had the bright lights and glamour of the Magic lifestyle overtaken what was true, valuable and lasting - a family? Was Victor going through a prolonged mid-life crisis and not able to buy a new red Corvette to satisfy it? Had Victor seen so much infidelity in his formative years that somehow this seemed to be an acceptable lifestyle? That the wives were accepting of adulterous relationships as long as they were taken care of by their men? Did I turn a deft ear because of fear of ending my dream? Had we fallen out of love? Had we lost respect?

I think all of the above have some merit. I was still concerned about Victor's emotional state. The two statements that Victor told me of his affairs were, "It was convenient," and "It was a release." When I asked Victor if he planned to leave home, his response was, "Why would I?" Imagine that, he probably felt he had the best of both worlds.

Only the fragments of a dream remained for me.

For Victor, it painted a portrait in vivid colors of what was important to him. He put on a good front that family was important, but as always, actions speak louder than words. Adultery tells children that their mother is worthless, and that their father's selfish desires take top priority.

There isn't a woman on earth who doesn't question herself after finding out that her husband was seeking fulfillment with someone else. I questioned myself, questioned my self-worth as a mother and wife, questioned if our whole life had been a lie and questioned how his family could have turned their back on this destruction. I constantly struggled with what could I have done to prevent this.

People justify and glamorize adultery, but no excuse or amounts of passion make it okay to destroy a family.

If the cost of your actions is your family, the cost is too high.

For someone like me who expected to marry only once and to share my life with only one man, this whole event was an unbelievable nightmare that I wished would end. To watch my dream and my family disintegrate was difficult to bear. The price of my love, commitment and trust should not have been deceit and destruction.

Fidelity is a given in a marriage — it should be expected. The lifeblood of a marriage should be respect. I used to wonder when people looked at me if they thought I should be wearing a big scarlet F on my chest - an F for Fool. Maybe I was a fool, and many whispered behind my back that I was in denial. That's a word that I take exception to. I don't think I was in denial, I just think I didn't know. I had never lived in or been exposed to a world in which spouses treated each other with so much contempt and disrespect. I didn't want to live in a marriage marred with doubt and suspicion. You don't marry someone expecting this sort of betrayal.

I didn't know all the lessons that God was about to teach me, but I knew I was on a spiritual journey that would explore the deepest elements of my being and I would never be the same.

We live in a world connected and affected by each other. Our actions have far reaching arms that touch people that might not even be born yet. We're dominoes, black and white and every color in between, stacked up so closely, that even a slight imbalance, a single tip, starts waves of toppling that sometimes never stops. Our children need two responsible parents living together, loving them and teaching them their place in the world. Our spouses need us to cherish the vows we pledged to each other seriously and sacredly. Spouses need to treat each other with not only love, but moreover respect. They are not just words but a lifelong commitment that is not made to be cavalierly broken. The vows we make are said to each other, but spoken before God.

* * *

I feel that not only does my husband have a personality disorder, but that he grew up witnessing duplicity in lifestyles, a disrespect for the institution of marriage and a warped sense of responsibility. He thought that as long as you provided for your family, i.e., financially, then he was entitled to do what he wanted. I believe that deep inside Victor knew that what he witnessed while growing up was wrong, and that little boy inside wanted something different for himself and his family once he had one. He tried hard to run from the patterns that he had seen and this caused the turmoil inside that ripped him apart. Eventually everything he ran from caught up to him because he had no firm foundation of morals and values to stand on.

Until we all realize that our world does not rotate on the axis of a single individual — until we take responsibility for our actions and the reactions they cause — until we take seriously our role in the line of dominoes, we cannot expect things to get any better. We will all, in some way, be like Victor - throwing it all away with no regard for the rubble we leave behind.

CHAPTER 9

Christ Begins With a Big C, cancer a little c

"A human spirit can endure a sick body, but who can bear it
if the spirit is crushed?"

Proverbs 18:14

Things were rough, to put it mildly. The responsibility of keeping a household together was more than over-whelming. I was beyond busy. It literally took from morning until late at night to run the household. Closer to the truth, it was running me. It took all the energy, organization, and perseverance that I could muster and then still, many nights I didn't get it all done. I would often pay the bills and do paperwork late at night because that was the time that was the quietest and I could concentrate a little, when I wasn't falling asleep.

The paperwork was phenomenal. There were always forms to fill out, notices to respond to, and junk mail to sort. Then there were the documents that needed to be changed to my name only, like car insurance, cell phone bills, and credit cards. I had never liked doing this part of the household duties, Victor had always done it, but there was no point in thinking about that now — I had to and I was going to.

Before Victor was arrested, I had been working pool on the 11-7 shift at Sand Lake Hospital. A "pool" position meant you filled in when they needed you and worked some holidays and summer vacations so the full-time people could take time off. After his arrest, I had to go back to nearly full time, working still at night so I could be available to the kids during the day. I hired a friend to sleep at the house during the night with the kids while I went to work — the things my husband used to. I would then come in around 6:00 a.m., just in time to get them up, feed them and get them ready for school. I'd drive them to school, come home, pray that Vic and Kelli wanted to take a nap in the next few hours so I could get some sleep before picking up the other kids from school. Then it would be time for homework, dinner, and maybe another nap before I went back to work.

There just wasn't time for the nervous breakdown that by now, I deserved to have.

It was grueling.

Those days are a very bad memory. They were filled with apprehension, fatigue and the unknown. I didn't know how my body would hold up and I guess I knew that it couldn't, but I was determined to do what I had to do. I remembered stories of single women who worked from day until night to support their families. I had heard these kinds of stories over the years, but now they were very poignant to me. I was one of them.

I don't think I have to say that I was tired. There is no term I can think of to describe how very tired I was, aside from excruciatingly tired. I was so tired that I hurt. As I drove home from work each morning, I would roll down the windows and stick my head out in the cool dawn air, forcing my eyes open long enough to get myself home. It was dangerous, I knew that I could wake up dead, or wrapped around a tree, but at this time, I felt I had no other options. I was numb.

I didn't feel right.

But who would feel right, working these hours, still nursing a baby, taking care of four other kids, while her husband was in jail. There was no time for my needs or my fatigue. I just had to do it. There was not room in my life at this time for my emotional or physical breakdown, so I just went on making a reason for every feeling that I felt. I had to keep going. I assumed, as I believe any woman in my position would have, that the way I felt was par and partial to the way my life was going at that time.

Nothing was right.

Including the lump I could feel at the top of my left breast. It did seem a little different from the other fibroid like lumps I'd had for years. But, I was nursing Kelli and assumed that the lump had something to do with that. It couldn't be anything - God haven't I had enough!! I kept telling myself that I couldn't be sick because I had just had a perfect pregnancy and a perfect delivery of a perfect baby girl. What 43-year-old woman could go through all that if she was sick?

Besides, I had absolutely no time to be sick. I was lucky to remember my name during these days, much less remember to make a doctor's appointment for myself. That was one extra trip that I didn't want to make. That was time for one extra nap that I could take. All my time needed to be to the kids and our life. Natalie was pretty much nothing more than a machine, doing what she needed to do to take care of her family. I was lost in the muddle of overwhelming grief and responsibility.

Hence, the mass on my breast was visible to the naked eye before I finally dragged my tired self into the doctor. In all honesty, in the state I was in, I could have had a mass the size of a grapefruit growing on the end of my nose, and I would have ignored it.

I went to the doctor on July 20, 2001.

I remember the day because it was the day before Victor's birthday and I had arranged a contact visit to take the kids and myself to see him. The kids had made him cards and we had put together a picture album for him. It was a nice visit. He was still in Seminole County at that time, awaiting sentencing. I was a little distracted the entire visit, because I knew of my pending doctor's appointment, but I didn't mention anything to him.

As soon as the doctor saw the lump he hurriedly began writing orders for a diagnostic mammogram and a surgeon for a biopsy.

"What do you really think this is, Doctor?" I asked.

He didn't look at me, but he did say that 80% of solid tumors are benign. That sounded good to me and I laid my hopes in that.

At first the mammogram was scheduled for a month away, and I couldn't imagine waiting that long. I had a good friend who was a radiologist, so I called her and asked if there was any way she could help me get an appointment sooner. I remember she called while I was at Water Mania with the kids and told me that she had an appointment scheduled for me two days later.

The doctor came in immediately after the ultrasound was over, and I had a strange feeling he was about to say something I didn't want to hear. My body retreated into some sort of a tunnel. It was like I was there, but far away from everyone else. It was like they were talking to me, but the words floated in the air like white-cottony dandelion seeds blown from a stalk. "It's a malignant tumor, needs radiation, chemo, looks like the lymph nodes are involved . . . " he droned on and on. And all I could say to myself was, "He can't be saying this to me. He can't really be saying this to me." But he was.

Didn't he know I have a husband in prison? Didn't he know that I was raising five kids alone and working at night? Why was he adding more to my already full plate? Haven't I had enough? Do I have to be sick too?

God, how much more will you ask me to bear?

His words started a whirlwind of medical tests and procedures that all started to blend into a massive blur.

I was in a new hell.

Wait a minute God! Haven't I had my share of misfortune?

I don't remember the exact order of all the things that followed. I had a lumpectomy and they removed 21 lymph nodes. Only three nodes were positive, so we hoped that it hadn't moved beyond the lymph nodes. I was scheduled for a bone scan and a test for the heart called a MUGGA, and an abdominal CAT scan. This scan and that scan to determine if the cancer had metastasized to any other parts of the body.

My mother was visiting again the day the call came in about the tests. My friend the radiologist called to give me the results. She said that the bone scan looked great. Something in the way she said it, I knew there was a "but" to follow. "But . . . I've got your liver scan here too and it's not as good. There's a lesion on your liver."

Granted, I didn't really know what that meant. I knew from her voice that it wasn't good. I knew that it being anywhere else was not good news. But, I didn't grasp what this news was saying to me. I didn't realize the fatality that a liver lesion implies. I told my mom that I had some good news and bad news. I just wanted her to hug me and tell me that it was going to be okay and to just let me have one big cry on her shoulder. I wanted to be her baby, but I knew that was not how she handled tough situations. So I toughened up, sucked it up and found a way to cope. When I told her it was only in my liver, she said, "Well, that doesn't seem so bad. At least it's not all over your body."

I agreed.

What we didn't realize is that, in actuality, it was all over my body. For it to reach the liver, it has to travel throughout the bloodstream.

The news was very, very bad.

I was scared, terrified —what new world was I entering?

Did I fall apart this time? Did I fall into bed and bury my head and weep and cry and mourn for my life? Yes, for a while. I went into the mode of "temporary life." I would not let myself plan for more than a month at a time. If I saw an outfit in a store that I wanted, I would say to myself, "I shouldn't invest in that, I might not be around to wear it anyway." If someone wanted to make plans for Christmas, I couldn't even talk about it because I feared that I might not be alive to see it. Whenever the subject of my children would come up, I would fall apart. I couldn't talk about my babies without breaking into tears.

I read somewhere that the average length of time for survival with liver lesions was 18 months, if you are lucky. My attitude was, I would just tread the water until then, not really living, just merely waiting on the end to be near.

Well, that got real old, real fast.

I got tired of dying and wanted to live. Life is about living. Whether it is two years, or two days, you've got to get the best out of each and every day. I decided I wasn't just going to survive anymore. No. I was going to beat cancer one day at a time. The day that I made that decision, I began to enjoy my life like never before. I had renewed energy and a zest to do as much as I could, for as long as I could.

No way was cancer going to take over my life.

I wasn't going to sit around and wait on it. It would have to catch me to kill me. I was going to buy that new outfit. I was going to get a pedicure when I could. I wanted to show my children that their mother was a fighter, and that she was going to live with cancer, not die by it. It just simply was not an option to die, not any time soon anyway.

Early on I realized that the diagnosis didn't matter. The prognosis didn't matter. What choice did I have? I wanted to keep on living. I had to still go on doing what I was doing — raising and loving my children and fighting for my life and my family. My options were limited, but I knew beyond a doubt that God would see me through — I just had to do my part and continue to have faith and believe.

Some of my dear friends and fellow believers held a healing service for me. We all prayed and cried and prayed and cried some more. I knew that everyone there was sincerely petitioning God for my healing. I drew a great deal of strength from this spirit filled service and really believed that I would be okay, no matter what.

People have asked what I did to deserve such hardships. Why was I singled out to endure such pain? I don't even venture to guess about such questions. My most common answer to people who view hardship as a punishment from God is, "Who was I to second guess what God's plan and purpose was for my life?" I'd ask them if they remembered that some of the greatest stories in the Bible were about people who endured incredible trials and in those hardships were brought even closer to God.

I had believed in His wisdom before, why should I stop now? More than anything else, it is clear to me that God is excessively patient with us. I believe that He wanted me to learn to trust in Him and only Him no matter what. I'd always been so independent, and able to do what I needed to do to take care of my family and myself. God was there, God was my helper, but I was the one in charge.

Even after Victor was arrested, I relied on God more, but I was always thinking, "What do I need to do to work this out? What do I need to do to help my kids . . . pay our bills . . . keep things rolling?" Again, I was helping God, instead of allowing God to help me.

I couldn't do that anymore.

Cancer took every "I" out of the question. I could no longer fix it. I could no longer work things out. I could no longer do anything but keep on living, keep on loving, keep on trusting a God who finally got my attention enough for me to hand over all the reigns into His ever capable hands, once and for all, and PRAY.

I remember telling Victor about the cancer. I called Seminole County and asked the guard on duty to ask him to please call me. I was driving in the car when the cell phone rang. It was Victor. I started to cry, and then blurted out, "I have breast cancer." He hesitated for a minute and asked me who told me that. I told him that I had been to the doctor, had a mammogram and they were sure. I envisioned him in his isolation cell with his head in his big hands and he cried a lot. I heard him cry uncontrollably for a few minutes and then started to rant with authority, "They can't keep me here, these walls can't hold me, these walls can't hold me!" Then through his tears, he asked me, "What else does our family have to go through?"

The whole scene was very sad and pathetic. It didn't make me think, "Oh, he really cares for me. He's really concerned about us . . . "

No.

Rather it made me want to shake him and scream at him and tell him that, in fact, they could keep him there, and they were going to. They were going to keep him there, for a very long time. The time for thinking about taking care of his family was long past. He had lost that opportunity, he threw it away out of foolishness, greedy stupidity or who knows what. But it was gone and it was not coming back, no matter how sick I was. If he thought things had been hard when he was free, he'd better hold on tight.

* * *

Nonetheless, shortly after my diagnosis, sentencing came. Victor was sentenced to 87 months in a Federal institution for dealing in counterfeit merchandise and drugs with intent to distribute. The judge said that she should throw the book at Victor but she had to consider his family's situation. She had been briefed about my health. I also spoke on behalf of Victor at his sentencing hearing.

Many of my dear friends were there for support and comfort. As I glanced at the faces of the people in the courtroom, some were a surprise to me when I saw them there. Others, I counted on being there, as they had always been. Many of them wept as I spoke. The judge was even visibly moved. I could hear their sniffles in the background as I spoke from my heart about what I think happened to my husband. Again, I asked, "Why was there so much energy spent on trying to get him, instead of trying to help him?"

I would still like to know. I began to hear that the department felt that he was beyond help. They felt he had a black heart. At the time, my feelings were that if there had been half as much effort spent on trying to rehabilitate this man who had so much promise, that it might have improved the odds of a better outcome for all involved. I felt this knowing that policemen are always a bit skeptical of rehabilitation and feel that the past most often predicts the future. I just wanted the prospect of the future to be a bit different, for my family.

I couldn't let go of the fact that here was a man with a good job, a good education, a half-completed Ph.D., and a family who loved him, and his future was to be spent in several different institutions until he ended up at the Federal Correctional Institution in Yazoo City, Mississippi. Something was so terribly wrong with this picture.

Despite the lack of answers, I had a definite peace on

this day and felt that God was nearby, as always. The judge gave Victor the lightest sentence that she could, considering the severity of charges against him. When the minimal sentence came, I thought it was an answered prayer. The judge said that she should have thrown the book at Victor Thomas, but she had to consider his family.

The task force thought it was a miracle that he didn't get more time, and were greatly disappointed. Everyone thought he would be sentenced to no less than 15 years. This would be something that I would never get a thank-you for from my husband. For Victor, I had served my purpose again.

But regardless of the shorter sentence, the reality remained the same — by his own actions and poor choices he was sentenced to a prison cell while his children grew up and his wife fought to live.

I began to believe that Victor was thinking that my diagnosis was his way out. My death would mean that I wouldn't be in his way anymore. He wouldn't have to sneak around. He could gracefully get out of all the drama of a divorce, and only temporarily have to pretend that he cared. I believed in his state of mind that he felt God had taken care of things for him. The only complication was, he wouldn't have a reliable, loving babysitter for the kids, while he ran the streets.

It probably couldn't come soon enough for him. He tried to discourage some of the alternative treatments that I was trying, such as acupuncture and herbal supplements. Once he told me that if he had cancer, he didn't know if he would do chemo. He probably said a prayer something like, "Thank you God for solving this whole thing for me."

Perhaps all this was another reason God moved him out of the way — to place into my life positive, sincere and encouraging people.

I was sentenced, virtually, to death. My first oncologist stood in the floor twice and told me that "I can't cure this." He wanted to make sure that I didn't have too much false hope.

I felt like saying to him, "You're only a physician, not the Great Physician. All I want you to do is your best and allow God to work through you if He chooses." I felt more depressed after my appointments with this doctor than from the thought of this horrible disease. He was insensitive and cold and I knew that I didn't need that. I thought, "I might be sick but I can still think and make decisions and one of my first decisions will be to leave you." I had already decided that when my chemo cycles were over, so would be our doctor-patient relationship.

My prognosis was poor. I couldn't accept that. I wouldn't accept that. I was in for the fight, no matter what, because I wanted to see my kids grow up and watch my grandchildren play. I wanted to be a grandmother! Now, when I saw people with gray hair, I felt jealous. "How lucky you are," I would think. What a gift you have been given - longevity. You have lived long enough to have gray hair and wrinkled skin. You are beautiful. I pray that I am as fortunate.

I stopped listening to stories of cancer patients who died. I stopped listening to the horror stories and grabbed onto the stories of hope, survival and triumph, because I was determined to be one of those stories someday. I didn't want to hear about any more of the death, destruction and betrayal that cancer can do to your body. Everybody knows that. I didn't want to look up another article on the internet if it was about dying. I wanted the against the odds stories. I didn't need any more negativity from Victor, the doctors, the scans, anything. I was looking to the future and not missing a step.

Please God, are you listening? I'm not ready!

I started my search for a soldier, a doctor who would help me fight and believe in the person that I was and not just another statistic. One who would join in the partnership with God and myself. I wanted one who believed in my life.

I needed a doctor who would look at me and look at my children and see that, "I had to be here."

Who would love and raise my children?

I knew that God would eventually lead me to the doctor that was right for me. The next doctor was more of what I was looking for, but not quite. I was still in search of that soldier. I decided to change doctors again, after consultations with other oncologists. I finally returned to a doctor who had a reputation of being an impatient fighter. I knew that we would make a good partnership. He is knowledgeable, impatient, a fighter, cutting edge and believes in "quality and quantity" of life. This was the doctor for me.

I realize that no matter what medical intervention I receive, this cancer might kill me in the end. I also realize that no matter what professional intervention or mentoring Victor might have received, his moral cancer might have destroyed him in the end too. But everyone deserves a fighting chance.

Subsequently, in September of 2001, I started chemotherapy, six rounds of the infamous adriamycin and cytoxin every three weeks. Three of my friends met me at the hospital for my first session, but I went to the rest of them alone. I would chat a little with the other patients there - I think I intended to be friendly, but distant. I talked to the nurses a lot, because I knew they would be there. I tended not to want to talk much or engage any of the other cancer patients.

I didn't want to get to know them or like them for my own protection - what if they weren't there the next time? I knew this wasn't the way to be, I had a lot to offer them, and they had a lot to off me, but I needed to save all my emotional energy for myself and the kids. Selfish, you might say, necessary, I might argue. Time after time, I couldn't get to know these wonderful people and lose them.

I just couldn't take any more loss

Chemo wasn't nearly as bad as I thought. Just before my

third round, all of my hair came out. I was completely bald. I didn't mind so much because my children didn't mind, and as long as I had their support, I could do anything. I invested in a couple of nice wigs, and bought some great hats, scarves and twists. I was never really down and bed ridden, or very nauseated. My white count never dropped too low for me to have to miss a cycle, and I never got an infection.

My children were awesome during this time. Many times they went to chemo with me. They weren't afraid, primarily because they didn't see me in pain. We'd sit and talk or watch television as the drugs infused into my body.

The nurses were very nice to my children and often offered to bring them a soda or cookies to munch on. The kids kept me going, emotionally, and physically. Thoughts of them helped me make it through. Sometimes they teased me about my bald head, and we'd all have a laugh. They just seemed to take it all in stride. Their favorite gesture was to bring me a glass of water before I went to bed.

Thank God for his hedge of protection. All in all, chemo wasn't as bad as I had heard it would be.

In April of 2002, I decided to have a liver resection to remove the cancerous lesion. I knew it was a big operation and had only been done experimentally with metastatic breast cancer patients, but I wanted to give myself any extra edge that I could. I talked to the surgeons and had my pre-op screening. I was ready for this, or so I thought.

Some of my friends and my parents met me at the hospital before the surgery and wished me well and prayed. "Mrs. Thomas, the nurses are ready for you." I said good-bye to my parents and friends and began the long walk down the hallway to the surgical prep area. "I'm going to be okay, I thought." At the same time they called me, they called another elderly woman. She didn't seem to have any family with her and truly looked alone. After taking a few steps down the hallway, her knees buckled. I stopped to help her up and assured her that she would be alright. She was sobbing and held onto my hand. They took the woman to another pre-op area and I never saw her again.

"Okay Natalie, keep it together," I said to myself. I got to my assigned bed and the nurses told me to change into the blue surgical gown waiting for me on the bed. With every piece of clothing I removed, the more I cried. By the time I was done changing and climbed into the bed, I was falling apart.

I was scared to death! I had prepared my will, taken care of the power of attorney, and done all I knew to do to make it easier on everyone, in case I didn't come back. Nonetheless, I was fear stricken.

God, you'd better come quick, 'cuz I'm not doing too good here. I wanted to go home! I didn't want to be here!

The nurse returned and asked me if I needed anything. I asked her to call the chaplain to pray with me. He came. I listened to him pray for exactly what I needed - peace and calm. I began to feel it. I too began to pray for God to be with me. I needed to feel Him now, in a hurry, before I jumped off this bed and went back to my children, my friends, my parents, my life!

My primary surgeon came in and asked me if I was okay. I told him, "No." He could see that I wasn't. He asked me if I still wanted to do this, and I told him yes, but I just couldn't shake the fear. He hurriedly wrote something in my chart and I knew he was writing orders for a sedative. I just kept thinking of my God, my children, my parents, and my dream - to be a grandmother.

Soon after, the nurse returned and explained that what I was feeling was natural. She told me that she had something to help me relax and I said, "Good," She soon put the medicine in my IV and I quickly relaxed and fell into a half sleep.

The next thing I remember is being wheeled into the

operating room and seeing one of the assisting surgeons who would soon have his hand inside my gut. He came over and introduced himself. That is the last thing I remember.

I woke up the recovery room to hear my surgeon and nurse discussing whether to remove my NG (nasal-gastric) tube or not. They did. My oncology nurse friend had come into the recovery room and said I told her that my back hurt. She said it was normal after laying flat for six hours. I was also doing well enough to not have to go to the intensive care unit.

God you are here. I panicked a little, but I knew you would come.

They removed 12% of the right lobe of my liver, the section that had the cancerous lesion. This was a major operation, and I had prepared to be in the hospital for at least 10 days. By the grace of God, I had no complications and was ready to leave the hospital in five days. I talked my doctor into two additional days of hospitalization for rest, after that, he said I had to go home, that there was no medical reason for me to be in the hospital.

Despite the surgery, the same God who had brought me this far, had poured out His grace and given me the strength to go camping with my Sunday school class in two and half weeks.

In June of 2002, I felt a tiny mass on the suture line of my lumpectomy. My surgeon believed it was scar tissue, but didn't want to take any chances, so he did a biopsy, and doggone it, the cancer was still there. You have got to be kidding! I wished this stuff would just go away and leave me alone. I wanted it to stop invading my life. In this same month, I had a bilateral mastectomy and a hysterectomy.

The doctors didn't want to do that radical of a surgery. My general surgeon was the same doctor who had done my liver resection and was always concerned about my welfare. He especially thought that it was just too much surgery and he tried hard to discourage me. I had grown to love him as a doctor and a friend, but this was one time that I needed him to understand that I needed to do this all at one time.

They felt it was overkill to remove a completely healthy breast, and they could shut down the function of my ovaries with drugs. I felt this was one time they needed to listen to me. I told them if I was going under anesthesia to remove one breast, they might as well remove the other, otherwise I'd be lopsided and just waiting on the other breast to generate more of these annoying mutant cells. And, since I was asleep, they might as well do the hysterectomy so I wouldn't have to take any additional drugs to stop the production of estrogen.

The removable of my breasts was not an emotional issue for me. They said they had counselors on staff to talk with women who were scheduled for mastectomies. No thanks. I had nursed five children and my breasts weren't exactly fit for a lingerie catalog. I actually sort of looked forward to some nice, new, perky breasts that were firm again. I could buy some cute little bras and with the right outfit, I might not even need one at all. If the removal of any of my body parts would give me a better chance at life, then I had no problem parting with them.

Again, when it was really time for the surgery and I was alone in that surgical prep area, I became very emotional. Two of my doctors came in after the nurse told them that they needed to go see me. My gynecologist and my general surgeon were very kind and reassured me. Again, I needed the drugs and the prayer to bring me the peace and calm that I so needed. There is just something about being alone in that surgical prep area that is so sterile, stark, and clinical that just devastates your peace and calm. You are alone and you know that only you can do this and you've got to dig down deep and pull out every bit of strength and resolve you have within yourself and pray to God to get you through it.

Nonetheless, they all felt I was going a little overboard, but I was insistent. I arranged all three doctors, the general surgeon who would remove both breasts, the gynecologist who would do the hysterectomy and the plastic surgeon who would do the immediate breast reconstruction. I had peace with my decision. I was out of the hospital in three days and white water rafting in three weeks.

Who says God isn't merciful?

For now, I keep on living. I set myself short-term goals and I meet them. I seek peace and comfort from God and I find it. I plan to keep going for as long as I can.

I'm tired.

I'm weary.

I believe the human spirit has a need for normalcy. It struggles to survive in spite of everything. I think that in spite of the betrayal, and in spite of the cancer, that God built within me and all of us, an innate spirit of victory. That is why we fight so hard to save what we have claimed - our families, our health and our relationship with God.

No matter what has been thrust into out lives, we draw on our need to overcome and reclaim our lives.

I wish that things were different. But they are not. My kids need me. They need me strong. They need me cheerful. They need me to teach them how to survive in adversity. They need me alive! Most of all they need to see that God had His hands on all of us and that He would continue to provide for all of our needs, just as He had up until now.

Perhaps, if Victor were at home, well I'd be approaching this all differently. Perhaps I would let myself sink into self-pity and fear. Perhaps I wouldn't have such a driving motivation to beat this thing if I felt that my kids had someone else to lean on. Or, perhaps God removed him so that I wouldn't have to fight for my life with the added aggravation of watching an unfaithful husband. Perhaps God knew that even all this couldn't change his heart. I don't know.

But, if having Victor gone helps me to rely more fully on God and allows my children to experience Him in a real way, then I am grateful for the way things are.

Much of my cancer battle is a very intimate and personal matter. Just between me and God. He walks with me every time I go into a hospital for a scan or to a doctor's office for a visit. He walks with me when I go for an injection or blood work. I gaze at the chemo patients as they have their spouse by their side and sometimes think, "My husband should be here with me." I allow myself to ponder that thought only briefly.

This kind of thinking is a one-way street for me. By allowing myself to wallow in these thoughts of what could have been, or moreover, what should have been, is to dig myself into an emotional hole that might be difficult to dig my way out of. That's when I turn it around and know that I am not alone. "He restoreth my soul." Some of my most intimate times with God have been during chemo or while waiting on a doctor's appointment. We have deep conversations when I am lying still and quiet in the MRI machine. Eventhough I don't enjoy having the scans, I have enjoyed this time with Him, and we have gotten to know each other so much better. These have been the times that He has poured out His peace and kindness and I have felt it more than ever. This is when I talk to God and rely on His presence. With Him, I am not alone.

Cancer is a battle of the emotions as you brace yourself to hear pathology reports from the doctors. There is such a sense of loss, of being out of control, and you are thrown into a world of technical talk, and test results, all in a battle for quality and quantity of life.

It is such an intimate battle to gather all the strength from deep within as you lie alone in the CAT scan or MRI machines one more time and know that it is looking in every crook and crevice in your body to find any of these cells that are raging war within your body. Your total thought is, "Please don't find anything." You battle your thoughts as you try to fend off the raging thoughts of, "What if the report is positive, what if they find something else?" "How will I handle it, what will I do?" God gets me through these times and again, I just remember that His plan is the perfect plan. I visualize my five beautiful children who need me and know that I have two of the greatest motivations in this world for waging all out war on this horrible disease - my God and my children.

These days, I do my scans and while I wait on my results, I live. I live every day to the fullest and tell myself that life is good, life is rich and that God is with me. It's not easy.

There are days when I'm low, but in the end, I have to believe and trust in the One who knows best. I can't be pulled down by the thoughts of what was, what should have been and what might be. " If you pray, don't worry, and if you worry, don't pray," as one of my girlfriends told me. It is so true. To do both of them is a waste of time, so why not just conserve your energy, and do the most effective one — pray.

I pray in my car, I pray in my bed, I pray in the bathtub. I pray in the day, I pray in the night, I pray whenever and wherever. There is not a perfect time or place, just a perfect One to pray to. I have learned to wait on Him, and rely on His guidance.

I seldom feel the need to worry anymore about what is around the corner. Although at times, it's a thought that permeates my peace. I know the possible realities, and they are so daunting that I readily leave the worry to Him. I say, "Here God, take my worries, they are too big for me."

Sometimes I would think about my own grandmother who had a battle with cancer. When I was about four years old, she lost the fight. I try to imagine what her thoughts were those many years ago, being widowed and raising three young children alone while fighting for her life, just as

I am. What would she say? What advice would she have given me? I have been told that her greatest regret was that she knew she would not live to see me grow up. She always felt so very close for much of my life. Sometimes if I was alone in a room, I would feel her behind me and think that if I could just turn around fast enough, that I would catch a glimpse of her. I don't have many memories of her, because I was so young when she died, but I have missed her too, and wish that she had lived long enough for me to get to know her.

I remember one morning dropping my son daughter off at school as I was on my way to the hospital to get my periodic scans. I had been feeling quite apprehensive, and was praying for a sense of peace. So far it hadn't come. I watched my little girl and boy happily hop out of the car with their backpacks bouncing on their backs and they ran along to school. They were so cute, so innocent, so precious and had no idea what was on my mind. I sat there for a minute in the car, in tears, as I watched them run through the gates of the school. Sobbingly I asked, "Please God, they are so young, so unsuspecting, I'm just selfish enough to not want them to be without me, or me without them. I want many more mornings of watching them grow, and seeing their backpacks bounce on their backs."

God are you listening? Please hear my plea!

I know God is faithful. He has provided so much beyond our basic needs. And His provision goes far above an intangible sense of peace and well-being. Though I may appear strong and able to stand on my own, He has woven an intricate web of individuals and actions that have been holding me up all along.

CHAPTER 10

I Am Not Alone

"Many beg favors from a prince; everyone is the friend of a
person who gives gifts!"

Proverbs 19:6

It only seems to happen in the middle of the night. I'm
jolted out of sleep by the strong arms of fear that grasp
my throat, making it hard to breathe. My heart begins to
pound so quickly and loudly that I'm sure it will wake one
of the children down the hall. On these nights the thoughts
come crashing in, one by one and then all at once. I feel like
I'm going to be crushed under their persistent pressure.

All of the strength and resolve that I wear as armor
throughout the day is stripped from my body and I lie in my
bed shaking, naked and afraid. On these nights I don't know
how I'm going to make it through another day. I don't think
that I can do it anymore.

Then quietly, surely, I feel the familiar tug that assures
me that I'm not alone. A peace pierces the panic like a single
ray of sun breaking through a foreboding rain cloud. I'm

reminded that I have the power to overcome whatever stands in my way. I have the promise by which I now live my life, that God will give me no more than I can bear. I get on my knees or call a friend to help me pray through it, and I say what I've said more in these past few years than I'm sure I said in all my forty plus years before . . . "I need to pray."

In spite of all the wonderful people who crossed my path, undoubtedly, I knew there were some who saw me as "different" now. I guess I made some people uncomfortable. I'm sure it was hard for people to make the adjustment to my new found situations. A few days ago, I was their peer, now I was living their worst fears. I used to be able to talk about the same things that they could talk about - houses, summer camps, a day at the spa, getting a new hair cut, a day of shopping at the mall. Now, life had changed for me.

There were those few who wanted to contribute and help out, but didn't care to invite me to their luncheons or parties. This was hard for me. I would hear about a luncheon, or a party and I wondered why I wasn't invited. What do you talk about with someone whose husband is in prison and who might be dead in six months? It began to make me profoundly appreciative of those who still saw me as worthy and vital. Those who were sensitive enough to know that I still had a need to be "normal."

I had to learn and accept that there would be those people who were afraid that what happened to me could happen to anyone at anytime. My situation was a little too close to home for some of them. I don't think people were being intentionally unkind or insensitive, I just think in many cases, they didn't know what to say or do, and then there were the few who just didn't want to get involved. They just didn't have the time to be bothered. Some people have a need to only associate with people that they perceive have attained a certain social status. I'm sure for some, I no longer fit this. Many times, I would break the ice and approach those who seemed standoffish, other times, I just let it go.

I probably have erected many walls around my emotions and my heart. I'm sure that I have. I might even now keep an emotional distance from people. My unconscious thoughts are probably to keep them away before they get close enough to betray and hurt me again. Sometimes it feels safer to be alone.

Just as the human spirit strives to survive, it also struggles to protect. I just hope that with time and prayer, I won't feel the need for this protectiveness.

Nevertheless, my life experiences have made me who I am. Thank God, I am precious in His sight.

God has shown me the best and the worst in people and sometimes it can be overwhelming. All of this is about trust. Trusting in a sovereign God who says, "Look Natalie, there are those who will feel uncomfortable with you now. But this is my sifter for your life. This will allow you to sift out who is for real and sincere. For the rest, just love them as I love them and leave the rest to me."

This reminded me of the summer the kids and I went mining for gems in the mountains of Tennessee. We were looking for rare and precious treasures to keep. We took a sieve and poured through bucket after bucket of sand, gazing intently at every speck, eagerly anticipating that rare find. In the end, we found only a very few gems that were bright and shiny. We were excited about these rare finds. Some of them were obvious and you knew right away that they had a different glow. They were a "keeper." Others, it was harder to see their real value. They were a little rough on the outside and you had to clean them up a bit and remove the silt and mud, to see what they were really made of. There were even a few that looked like they might be a rare find, but crumbled into pieces when you pressed them between your fingers.

Friendships are that way, when God places those

sincere, valuable, through thick and think, rare finds in your life, they are "keepers." For some, the rest, you have to let them go back to the mud and silt where they were and allow God to refine them into those rare gems, in His time.

You will hear that chivalry is dead. That everyone is just out for themselves, or for what they can get out of life. It's only "me, me, me." I used to believe that, but I have learned first hand that in addition to the "keepers" there are many giant-hearted, selfless servants out there who go above and beyond the normal call of duty.

My children attend the First Academy, a private Christian School sponsored by First Baptist Church of Orlando. Within the school's PTF, there is a ministry called Samaritan's Heart that was created to serve TFA families in special times of need. This ministry sent a letter out to TFA families within weeks of Victor's arrest, asking for help with meals, car pooling, home cleaning services, errands, light babysitting, grocery store gift certificates, school uniforms, and emergency monetary assistance. The outpouring of generosity was nothing less than miraculous. Anyone who felt the call, had a place to help that fit them perfectly. To quote a TFA friend of mine, "I've seen TFA reach out to help before, but never like this."

In time, because our needs were ongoing, a trust fund was formed. The headmaster of the school, a man who became one of my dearest friends, and a trusted confidant, actually agreed to be trustee of the fund on my behalf. This way, I would not have to worry about any of the details, and also to assure that anyone who felt led to contribute would know that not a penny of it would be spent on Victor. Some were concerned about this, their intent was to help me and the kids, but not the man who put us in this situation.

One of the reasons that my children were able to handle this crisis so well, and still be socially active, was because enough people felt in their heart a desire to help provide a measure of normalcy and consistency for the children that would not have been there otherwise.

Providing for our meals and other details of life was huge. But, it was nothing compared to what these dear people were called to do after I was sentenced with cancer. The reality of my situation, the fact that I had no idea how I was going to care for my children through the battle was so unfathomable that I could hardly bare it. I had always wanted to be a mom and prided myself in taking care of my children, and now it seemed as if this was going to be taken away from me, temporarily anyway. I knew my parents had physical limitations because of their own illnesses.

I knew in my heart that God was there with me, but I could not see how I was going to keep everything together while fighting this thing. There were people who understood what I was about to go through. It seemed as though everyone knew someone in the battle with cancer, and knew that I was going to need HELP. I remember the day I sat the kids down to tell them of my illness, in the same place I sat them down to tell them about their father's arrest. I promised them then that I would always be there for them. How was I going to live up to that promise? How could I stand to let these children down again?

I didn't have to.

When my illness became known among the organizers of Samaritan's Heart, they decided that what I needed was a full-time nanny and helper. Within days of the idea's inception, they found out that a young woman was returning to Orlando, fresh with a social work degree. She was looking for a job as a nanny to help pay off some student loans. When she found out about my need, she felt that God had called her to help.

But how to pay her?

Gina, a dear woman, who I admired and always saw the work of God in everything, wrote a proposal to a charitable organization in town, hoping to secure between \$25 - 30,000 for a one-year salary. The proposal was denied because the organization did not want to start a precedent of funding things of this nature.

Frustrated but not defeated, we all began to pray for God's will. Within days of the denial, two separate families from the First Academy donated enough money to pay the entire salary. This lesson in faith was reinforcement to learn to trust Him. Now I had someone to watch Vic and Kelli during the day, help with getting them fed after school, help with housework and laundering when needed, and cook . . . all the things I would no longer be able to do. She enabled me to focus on getting better instead of merely surviving. She helped put me back on my feet after the surgeries and the chemo rounds.

I am sure that the demands of a large household were a bit overwhelming sometimes, for such a young woman. I have no doubt that she was completely exhausted. I can't apologize, because after the year we had been through, I needed the emotional break. This young woman provided that. I couldn't have done it without her. She was an angel to me.

There were many.

That first Christmas with Victor gone and me in the midst of chemo, with no hair and no husband, I had little hope for a joyous holiday celebration. I didn't even want to try. I had not put up a decoration or sent out a card. I had not bought a present or baked a cookie. I didn't have the resources to buy what I wanted or the energy to make everything seem all right. In my heart, Christmas was just something I wanted to avoid this year.

I wanted to escape, take the kids, leave our home, get away from Orlando, and take a Christmas vacation, to possibly distract me from the holiday that was just around the corner.

"Natalie, do you have a Christmas tree yet?" one of the

teachers from the school called and inquired. "Well no," I replied. "Well, just stay there and I'll be over in about an hour," she explained. "Okay, see you soon," I responded.

In about an hour, she was at my front door with one of the most beautiful trees that I had ever seen. It was nothing short of perfect. She marched right in when I opened the door and set up the tree in the stand that she had brought. It all went without a hitch. When she was finished, she stood up and asked, "Now do you want me to decorate it?" I mused at the thought, but knew that Christmas was going to come to our home. My children and I would love to decorate this heaven-sent tree.

I learned for the first time what Christmas was really meant to be. It wasn't about me, or about how I felt, or about what I would be able to put under the tree. It was about a selfless gift of love, given to an undeserving world in the most humble of settings. It was about a God who knew exactly what was needed and how to fulfill those needs - even if it wasn't the way the world expected.

Christmas came to my house that year, like never before.

By the time school was out for Christmas vacation, gifts started pouring in. There were gifts for all of the children - many of the things they had asked for and so much more. In fact, we received so many gifts that we were able to give some to other families in need, allowing my children to experience the joy of giving and seeing the grateful responses from those who receive. It was a blessed time. God was and is so good.

How could I ever forget the sweet souls that helped make our Christmases joyous? The kids and I were in the worst situation in our lives, but it was during this time that we learned the real meaning of Christmas through the servants that God sent to bring us joy.

There were Sunday school classes, Brownie troops, and social organizations.

I can recall the stories of the many people who sent meals to my home after my husband was arrested, and the many more that were sent after the Christian community learned that I was battling cancer. I love to remember the mothers who volunteered to "fill up the freezer" so that there would always be food in the house for the children.

It makes me humble to relay the story of the couple who deposited money they had saved for a family vacation into our trust fund. I was told they felt that whatever they had, came from God and they wanted to share their blessings with someone else.

We couldn't have done without the thoughtful people that dropped off used clothing, uniforms and furniture. I'm indebted to the moms who took extra care to remember my children's birthdays and offered to make sure they had cupcakes in the classroom if I didn't feel well enough to do it. History was recorded by the parents who took the extra time to take pictures of my kids at field trips and special school events when they knew I wasn't able to be there.

The sheer kindness of others. All my friends new and old who kept vigil at the hospital when I had my surgeries. They prayed as the surgeon's scalpel parted my flesh. I'll never forget your faces when I opened my eyes in the recovery room - you were more of a comfort than you will ever know.

There was the former oncology nurse who had formed a ministry just for cancer patients. She was wonderfully comforting and always full of hope.

Then the families from another church who stepped up to help. They were so kind - they barely knew us but felt a call to help.

The families who walk beside us day by day. Who make that call just to see how we are, or to say, "I just called to see if you needed some help." They are there to help at a moment's notice.

All these and other contributions were invaluable in

every way. You all made such a difference in our lives. There aren't many times in this life when you know that your actions have made a real difference to someone - please know that you make a huge difference in the quality of life of six people.

It's hard to even communicate the gratitude I have for the multitudes of people who stepped into the doors of my life. It sounds like a cliche, but words cannot express how I feel. I know that I will never be able to repay or even thank with words most of those involved. But I also know that they did not do it for thanks or recognition from me - they wished to respond as the Lord placed the call on their hearts. They gave from deep within, no strings attached. We wouldn't be where we are today, without the kindness and generosity of others.

Faithful souls were there to help with the kids, listen to my cries, and take care of the little things that can turn into big things when left unattended for too long. They prayed for me, interceded on my behalf, and those prayers have been answered again and again. I never saw much of what went on for me, especially in those first few days of the outreach for support, but I knew my friends were there - and they are my friends whether I have met them or not.

Through the efforts done on our behalf, we were deeply blessed, as were the many people who served us. For the first time, many of us were able to see what the church, and real friendships were really meant to be. It was phenomenal and astonishing, and all God!

The church was created to be the hands of Jesus after He left earth to sit once again at the right hand of His Father. It's purpose is to serve, to give, to love, to sacrifice, to perform miracles, even the smallest of miracles, just as Christ had done while walking amongst us.

That's what it did for us.

Often we approach church wondering what we can get

out of it. How will it fulfill our needs? How will it serve us? But, that's not how it's meant to be. The church isn't the building, the pastor, the sermons, or the singing of hymns. It's not the programs or the passing of the plate. The churches are the people, doing what Jesus would have done in love and grace. Of all the things I am thankful for, being able to have experienced the church to this depth and magnitude has enriched my life beyond belief.

I pray every day that neither my children nor I will ever forget what was done for us. I pray that we will be different, and better people because of the sacrifices that many gave. I pray that we will never grow complacent or complaining or expectant . . . but that we will forever understand the meaning of sacrificial love.

Some of us are so hesitant to accept help. Some of us want to do it ourselves or do without. It is a hard lesson for some of us to learn how to receive. By denying others the gift of serving us, we are denying God His plan. When others serve us, it is not about us, it is about God. Don't squelch what God wants to do through others. As my dear friend Ed once told me, "I didn't love you until I served you."

More of us are hesitant to give. We would use excuses like, we don't know what to do, or we thought it was being taken care of. I used to be that way. But, what we must realize is that by serving others, we are allowing God's purpose to be fulfilled in their lives. We all have something to give or something to do for others.

I have met some incredible servants along this journey. People that live by the scriptures and know how to give, love, encourage, pray and serve. They do what is placed on their hearts in spite of me. In spite of my pride, my objections to their help and my floundering independence. They have learned what God wants all of us to learn - to do what Jesus would do.

The guiding verse for the Samaritan's Heart Ministry is Ephesians 2:10, "For we are God's workmanship, created in Christ Jesus to do good works, which God prepared for us to do." It has become one of my guiding verses as well, for I never want to miss out on the opportunities to serve Him in the lives of those in need. Above and beyond! All God!!

CHAPTER 11

No More Than I Can Bear

"And God is faithful; He will not let you be tempted
beyond what you can bear. But when you are tempted,
he will also provide a way out so that you can
stand up under it."

I Corinthians 10:13

"**M**om, don't forget I have basketball practice today".
. . . "Mrs. Thomas, we have you scheduled for scans
tomorrow at 8:30". . . . "Natalie will you be able to attend the
grade level meeting this afternoon?" . . . "Mom, the toilet is
clogged again!". . . . "Mrs. Thomas, the brake job on your van
will be $813.57" . . . "Mrs. Thomas, just a reminder that the
children have a dental appointment tomorrow" . . . "Natalie,
the money in the trust fund is getting very low" . . . "Mrs.
Thomas, your will is ready for review" . . . "Mom, we're
hungry!"

"Hey, God wait a minute! Are you sure you have the right
person for this job? Can I do this? You said you wouldn't give
me more than I could bear, but isn't this pushing it a little bit?

I don't feel like I can stand under this. God, are you sure you have chosen the right woman?

I need to pray. Lord, I need you beside me. Jesus help me! My spirit starts to settle.

As I listen to the wispy, rhythmic breathing of my little daughter sleeping next to me, I realize two things.

That I have done nothing that God has not been in control of.

I am nothing without Him.

It had been His will and His plans that guided me through this maze called life. God cleared the path for me when I didn't even know it. He was there all along. Not one detail had been missed, not a step mistaken.

". . . He will also provide a way out so that you can stand up under it." Therein lies my strength. God never promised us it would be easy. It hasn't been. But, He has been so true to His promise, that He would help us bear it. I have seen that in my life. I have felt His presence so intensely, especially when I was in my lowest valleys.

As I look back on events in my life, I can clearly see the hand of God pruning and shaping my life. He was slowly strengthening me to handle what He knew I would one day face.

Everybody likes a happy ending — myself included. We want to read a story and come to the end to see how everything worked out rosy and right.

There's not a happy ending to this story.

Not yet.

I don't know how it will end. It is one of the many questions I carry around with me on a daily basis. What if this? What if that? What if . . .

There are many unknowns. But there are many things I know as well.

I have gotten over the man. I have gotten over the marriage. I have gotten over the loss of a dream. The things that I wanted in the first chapter of my life story were not the things I wanted at the end. I have grown and grown up.

But, I am not unique. God has given many people difficult trials. Those who make it are those who trust and believe in Him enough to give Him total control of their lives. He doesn't want 51% or 99%. He wants us to trust our entire lives, 100% to Him. This is where I came face to face with my toughest battle of all.

I knew that my children belong to God. They were a gift - a loan. I had given them to Him many times over in prayers, but I had always taken them back. This had always been my private struggle with God. I have trusted Him with my health, my marriage, my finances, everything. But I have yet to trust Him completely with the beings that were closest to my heart - my children - His children.

God blinded me to so many painful things. I knew that the children had been the deepest source of my anger with Victor - that he not only betrayed me, but betrayed five precious beings that did not deserve it. I still hold so much anger because of this. I am angry for my children.

I didn't like who I was with Victor Thomas. I stayed needy, and insecure. I always second guessed myself. I knew I was better than that. I was ready and able to take charge of my life, for myself and my children.

Still, I just wanted to yell at him, "Was it worth it?" "Why couldn't you get control of yourself and your life for their sake?" "Couldn't you have been circumspect about your actions enough to think of your children's welfare?"

Love . . . honor . . . morality and trust are all choices. Without trying, we model our values. It is our job as parents to demonstrate to our children what is important and valuable. We cannot validate bad behavior. That is the sickness and the sin.

In short, I do not know if I will beat this cancer. Statistics say I won't. Some doctors say I won't. But I have hope that one way or another, things will work out for the best. For now, I am doing all I can to stay healthy. I eat well, I go to the doctor and get all my pokes and prods and scans whenever I am supposed to. Great strides are being made to increase the life spans of women like me.

I will not be beat by cancer. I am not saying I will not be killed by cancer. I am realistic about that possibility. But I will not be beat by it. I will not live my life as a cancer patient. I will not succumb to the fear and doubt and negative prognosis. I am going to live. I am going to breathe. I am going to get up every morning, not wondering if the cancer is back, but wondering what I'm going to do to live up to my purpose in this life. Even if I do one day die of this beast, I will know without a doubt that "I have fought the good fight, I have finished the race, I have kept the faith." (2 Timothy 4:7). It will not beat me.

Looking back, I know that there were many times I should have put myself first. I should have kept my doctor's appointments, and I shouldn't have ignored the prescription for the mammogram that my doctor gave me. I owed it to my children to take care of myself. To make sure that I kept myself in good health to be here for them.

Will my kids survive this ordeal without being severely scarred? Will they suffer consequences into their adult lives for the sins of their father and mother? I don't know. Spiritually, "If God is with you, who can be against you?" With Christ, they have an opportunity, to make better, wiser, Godly choices. That has been an important thread in this fabric of life - choices.

My children were fine. They were doing quite well in school, happy, optimistic, but realistic. They loved to play, participate I sports, talk, socialize with friends, and go to church. They do not live their life in fear either. I knew that if they had to face their future without me, that they would be okay. I knew from their conversations that at least they knew they had a future. That was important to me. I was relieved to know that they hadn't lost hope in their own lives and weren't being smothered by negativity and doubt. No matter what, they would have each other and an awesome Heavenly Father.

Nonetheless, people ask me if I feel that marrying Victor was a mistake. I usually pause for a moment before I respond. Then one of my children will break the silence and the answer becomes an easy one. When I look at my five jewels, I know that they were not a mistake. They could never be a mistake. They are so unbelievably precious that sometimes when I think of the possibility of not being with them, it takes my breath away.

Victor and I made some terrible mistakes in our lives. But if playing a leading role with him in this tragic melodrama produced five of God's greatest blessings, then the pain of the relationship was worth it.

When I go to chemotherapy, they deliver the medicine through a port that lies just underneath the skin on my chest. The port has wires that go to my heart, so the medicine that might prolong or save my life can be delivered throughout my body. God is trying to deliver His life blood of grace and mercy directly into all of our hearts in the same way. Through the chemotherapy medicines I have a chance at life. Through the grace of God, we all have an abundant life that is promised to us. For the chemotherapy medicines, I lie still and submit to the medicine that is given to me. For the grace of God we remain still and peaceful and rely on Him to give us just the right amount of His love to sustain us. I trust Him, I believe in Him and I know that He will never fail me.

My kids and I are a family, a strong family and have a lot of love for each other. I did not drive my husband to make the choices that he made. My children did not drive their father to make the choices that he made. Victor drove his own decisions, with little thought of anyone except

Victor. Victor's ambitions had nothing to do with God - only Victor. According to one psychologist, "His apologies should be the size of Texas." Unfortunately for Victor's soul, they usually only amounted to a line or two and weren't very palpable.

I tried to see the best in Victor Thomas. I would have gone the distance with him. I don't regret this, for it is the true meaning of unconditional love. He took advantage of my devotion to him. This was a man who abused his role in the relationship, and my illness. He eroded the very basis of a marriage. How dare he? What gave him the right to take away my dream just because he no longer shared it?

Just as I learned to let go of my dream, I turned my hand to God and knew that He had the foresight and hindsight to know what was best for my life and that of the children He so generously trusted me to raise.

Now, I better understand the priority of life, my God before any man. If you put your trust in man, they will disappoint you every time. They don't always mean to, they are just being people. As one of my oldest girlfriends told me long ago, "If it isn't rooted in faith, then it won't work." She was so right.

Many people live their lives trying to forget the past. For me, the past held many answers and unlocked doors to answers that I needed to go on with my life. I had found a person that I liked again - me. And I have risen above the image that Victor Thomas tried to impose on me. What I do not accept is that my husband's actions were my fault. Victor wanted me where I was. He wanted me down, and acting out because in his mind, it justified his own actions. He had the excuses he needed, to do what he wanted. Living by your wants only keeps you happy in the short run. In the long run of life, you have to keep your focus on Jesus.

I had gained my peace of mind that was lost so long ago. With the circumstances that I have experienced, I will always carry certain scars when it comes to trust. Although I have found peace with this emotion, I don't think it is buried very deep below the surface. I am not sure trauma of this magnitude ever completely goes away. You learn to pray, find peace and move on with the grace of God.

I do not want to be caught up in looking back. I don't want to lose what I have right now in the present, by living in the past. My future is ahead of me.

* * *

Lord God, protect my children.

My greatest heartbreak of all, would be if my children lived out some of this calamity all over again. This was not the life I wanted for them. As they craft their own lives, I hope that they will learn from the mistakes of their parents, not repeat them. I try to tell my children about me and my share of mistakes. I do this because I believe that family secrets hurt. If my children do not know the truth, they will inevitably repeat it. I want their touchstones of strength to be found in a reliance on God.

* * *

Now the other life seems so long ago.

Sometimes I wish I could turn back the hands of time and change all this nonsense.

Now my battles have taken on a different meaning. Not driven by anger or rage. Not consumed with doubt and lack of faith.

Living life as an Unbeliever is like driving a car without a steering wheel. You have nothing to give you guidance through life. You start the car and think, "I've got it." You waver and veer to the left and then back to the right, never getting in control of the road of life. Whoops, you get over that bump in the road and you think you've got it made. But, what about the next tree and the hairpin turn? How will you guide yourself without help? After you've had enough, you start to be convinced that you need a higher power before you go over the edge of the cliff and can't make it back. Now the road gets curvier and narrower. You feel totally out of control and you shout, "God, I need you!!" He is there - He always has been.

He takes control and gives direction. He gives us the guidance we need to negotiate the twists and turns on that unpredictable road of life.

It all makes sense again.

I'm not saying that I know all the answers. My experiences don't make me think that I have it all figured out and still have nothing to learn. I still have a lot to learn. I don't feel self-righteous, or self-absorbed.

I saw a bumper sticker once that said, "Being a Christian doesn't make you perfect, just forgiven." That's what I feel - not perfect, not all knowing, not better than anyone else, just forgiven when I act all too human.

I just know that there are times in our lives, albeit painful, you have to let people go who bring pain, and self-doubt into your life. God doesn't expect us to stand by and time after time allow someone to abuse and mistreat us. There is a difference in turning the other cheek and holding someone accountable who does wrong.

* * *

I pray that I am able to forgive my husband in the way that God would have me. It has been a difficult journey to unqualified forgiveness. I am not there yet. The hardest thing is to forgive people who knowingly bring destruction to your life, and to realize that they don't care. I have to let go of this - God expects me to, and I want to glorify Him.

Could I have seen things any differently? Certainly, if I had been open to the murmurings of God. He tried to show me things, but my heart wasn't as open. There is no doubt, I wish many things in my life were very different. But the question remains, would I have allowed God to work so magnificently in my life if things had worked out differently?

Ultimately, the only thing I knew for sure in this crazy world that turns itself upside down in the blink of an eye, or the answering of a cell phone call, was that God's promises were real and true. He had brought me through this, taught me through this, and had grown me through this. I became a better person because of these trials. I became the best that I had been in many years, maybe ever. Romans 8:28, an old familiar verse that I've heard over and over through the years, has become much more than words on a page, "And we know that in all things God works for the good of those who love him, who have been called according to His purpose."

I continue to pray, believe, and have faith. I continue to serve Him to be thankful for the wonderful people that He has brought to my life. I love my parents and accept them for who they are. We are all products of our life's experiences, therefore all of us love in our own way, the way that we know how. I continue to enjoy my children and the life that God has woven for us. For me, the darkness is gone and except for brief periods, the apprehension of what might lie ahead has been put to rest.

My life has become similar to the spokes of a wheel. Each spoke working in synchrony with the other. My God, my children, my friends, my parents, my church, the kids' school, and all those who so unselfishly followed the will of God as He placed us on their hearts. All extending from the center and held together by a God who formulated such a perfect plan that they work harmoniously to bring glory to Him.

On conclusion, looking back, after putting the pieces back together, I finally get it. I now understand not only in

my head, but in my heart, and it has become my life song, "
. . . and God is faithful; He will not let you be tempted
beyond what you can bear. **But when you are, He will also
provide a way out so that you can stand up under it."**
(I Cor 10:13)

Focus on Jesus. Trust Him.

Epilogue

In the summer of 2003, the cancer returned to my liver. I resumed another round of chemotherapy which worked well and erased all tumors except one. At this time, that one remains dormant. My thanks again goes to the Great Physician himself. All in all, the doctors were pleased with the results. Now I remain on an oral chemotherapy. I still have a great quality of life with my children.

My focus remained the same - my God and my children. They are the constant in my life.

* * *

All of us have a capacity to give. Reach out to others who are less fortunate. Stop making excuses or being fearful of not having enough for yourself. God will provide for you. I once heard an analogy that many of us have our fists closed so tight, trying to hang onto what we have, that we won't open it long enough for God to put more into it.

Give, help, encourage and pray for others.

"Each of you should look not only to your own interests, but also to the interests of others." (Phillipians 2:4)

Subjects and Corresponding Scriptures

When we have any doubt about the direction of our lives, we can always return to the Words that He left to guide us. Here are some of the scriptures that I have used during my journey.

The subject is listed, along with a corresponding book, chapter and verse from the Bible. The Lord's Word is the truth and will make our paths clear as we follow Him.

1. **Adultery**   Hebrews 13:4; Exodus 20:14; Mark 7:20
2. **Children**   Proverbs 20:7; Proverbs 20:11; Isaiah 11:6
3. **Death**   Psalm 89:48; Proverbs 18:21; Proverbs 11:19
4. **Deceit**   Mark 7:22; Romans 1:29; 1 Peter 2:1
5. **Faith**   Matthew 6:30; Romans 5:1; Psalm 85:11

6. **Forgiveness**   Psalm 19:12; Psalm 65:3;
                      Colossians 3:13
7. **Healing**   Psalm 103:3; Jeremiah 17:14;
                      Isaiah 53:5
8. **Love**   Deuteronomy 11:1; Chronicles 16:34;
                      Psalm 85:10
9. **Repentance**   Jeremiah 15:19; Ezekiel 18:30;
                      2 Peter 3:9
10. **Trust**   Psalm 28:7; Psalm 33:21;
                      Proverbs 11:28

Bibliography

Vaknin, Sam. "Narcissistic Personality Disorder (NPD), Definition, Fact Sheet and Tips." <u>Malignant Self Love - Narcissism Revisited.</u>, second, revised printing (1999. 2001). <htttp://www.samvak.tripod.com>.

Freeny, Michael. Michael Freeny Associates. Telephone interview. October 2003.

Federal Bureau of Investigations. Surveillance transcripts. October 1999 - March 2000.

Lancaster, Cory. "Orange Gets Tough With Young Criminals, Officials Will Soon Launch A Program To Hunt Down And Round Up Juvenile Offenders." <u>Orlando Sentinel</u>. 18 Jan. 1998: Local and State.

Lucado, Max. <u>The Great House of God</u>. Dallas, TX: Word Publishing, 1997.

Printed in the United States
26134LVS00001B/415-441

9 781594 674501